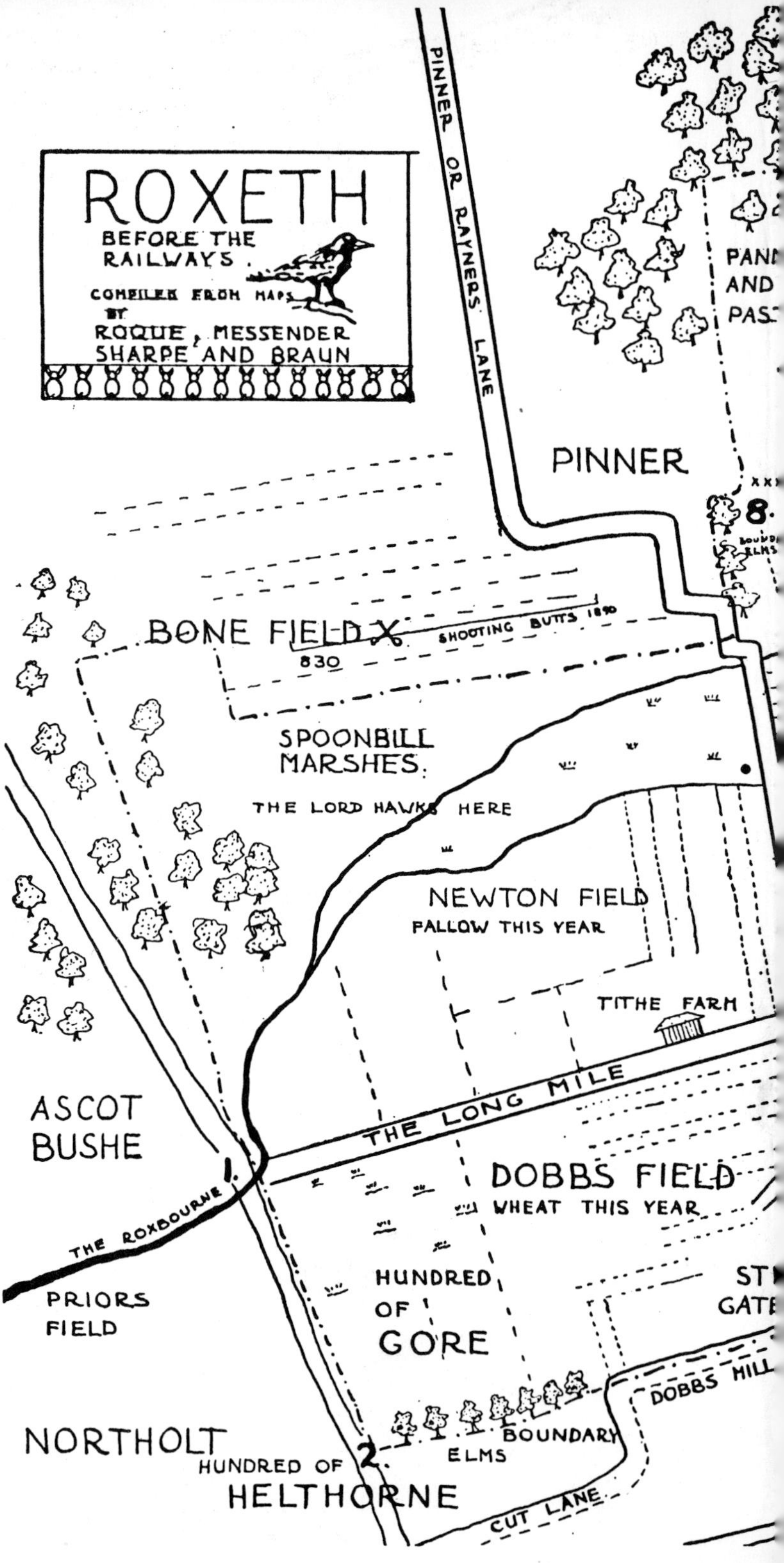

ROXETH BOUNDARY MARKED —·—·—   STONES ARE NUMBERED.

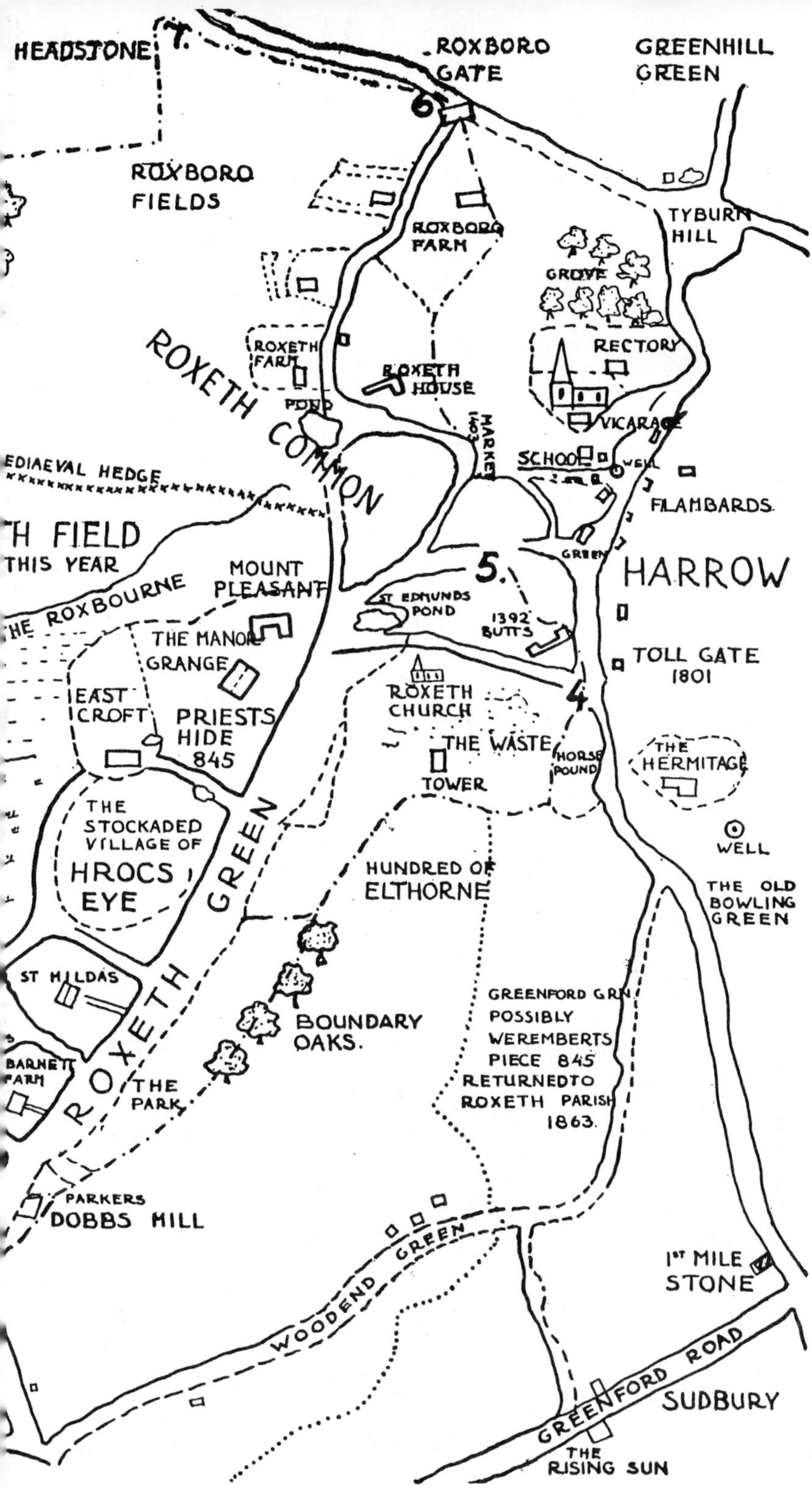
HEADSTONE
7.
ROXBORO GATE
GREENHILL GREEN
6
ROXBORO FIELDS
ROXBORO FARM
TYBURN HILL
GROVE
ROXETH FARM
ROXETH HOUSE
RECTORY
ROXETH COMMON
POND
MARKET 1403
VICARAGE
SCHOOL
WELL
EDIAEVAL HEDGE
FLAMBARDS
H FIELD
THIS YEAR
GREEN
5.
HARROW
MOUNT PLEASANT
THE ROXBOURNE
ST EDMUNDS POND
1392 BUTTS
THE MANOR
GRANGE
TOLL GATE 1801
EAST CROFT
PRIESTS HIDE 845
ROXETH CHURCH
4
THE WASTE
HORSE POUND
THE HERMITAGE
TOWER
THE STOCKADED VILLAGE OF
HROCS EYE
WELL
HUNDRED OF ELTHORNE
THE OLD BOWLING GREEN
ST HILDAS
ROXETH GREEN
GREENFORD GRN
POSSIBLY
WEREMBERTS
PIECE 845
RETURNED TO
ROXETH PARISH
1863.
BOUNDARY OAKS.
BARNETT FARM
THE PARK
PARKERS
DOBBS HILL
WOODEND GREEN
1st MILE STONE
GREENFORD ROAD
SUDBURY
THE RISING SUN

ROXETH
845
A.D

THE STORY OF ROXETH

by
T. L. Bartlett

London Borough of Harrow
1992

First published 1948
This edition specially produced
by
Cedric Chivers Ltd, Bristol
for the publishers
The London Borough of Harrow
Education Department Library Service
Civic Centre, Harrow HA1 2UU
1992

ISBN 0 901034 15 0

Printed in Great Britain by
Cromwell Press Ltd, Broughton Gifford, Wilts

FOREWORD

by Dave Bartlett

My father, Tom Bartlett — known to different groups as T.L.B., Tom or Skip — mentioned to me about the Phoenix rising from its own ashes while he was writing this book. When past heritage and traditions seem to have been stamped out and lost forever, a remnant returns.

He would be overjoyed to know that his book was being reprinted, especially because of the interest of schools and libraries. Some of his happiest moments were spent revealing to parties of children the wonders of creation and the secrets of the past.

The concern and enthusiasm he had for 'Old Roxey' will continue amidst all the changes. I welcome the opportunity of giving the family's blessing to this second edition, and my thanks go to Harrow Library Service, and to Roxeth Local History Society for helping to organise this production.

I trust it will encourage all those who now endeavour to keep the 'Rooks of Roxeth' alive, by relating the history of its peaceful pastures to all who value the heritage of the locality wherein they dwell.

POSTSCRIPT

It is a great privilege to be asked to write a postscript to this reprint of 'The Story of Roxeth'. To me it is a book of great charm as well as scholarship. The love that Tom Bartlett had for the Roxeth of his youth is reflected throughout its pages and indeed is the great strength of the book.

Those who only know present day South Harrow may wonder at Bartlett's enthusiasm for a place that had all but disappeared, even in name, by the time 'The Story of Roxeth' was published in 1948. In the following 20 years the great barn and the moated Roxeth Grange, the Parish Hall, The Three Horseshoes pub and all the cottages that lined Northolt Road from Roxeth Corner to South Harrow Station were demolished and replaced by featureless office blocks and flats. So today there is even less tangible evidence of the Roxeth that Tom Bartlett described so eloquently.

Yet both the name and the spirit of Roxeth stubbornly refuse to die. Bartlett's 'Friends of Roxeth', responsible for the first publication of this book, was eventually succeeded by the 'Roxeth Research Group'. In 1984 that group produced another memorable book — 'Roxeth Remembered'. Charles Gee, the late Ron Pratt and Albert Tickner, all old Roxonians, proved worthy successors to Tom Bartlett in that exercise.

Such was the revived local interest that followed the formation of the research group that it was a natural development for Roxeth Local History Society to be formed and we celebrate our first ten years of continuous activity in September 1992. There is also a two-day annual Roxeth Show held in Roxeth Recreation Ground and a local government ward named Roxeth.

So it can be seen that since 'The Story of Roxeth' was first published many people have striven to keep the name of Roxeth in being and to retain that elusive spirit of Roxeth. Tom Bartlett lit the flame, I am sure this reprint will keep it burning for the current and future generations of Roxonians.

David Gibbons
Chairman
Roxeth Local History Society

THE STORY OF
ROXETH

BY

T. L. BARTLETT, B.A.
M.B.O.U.

Published for
'The Friends of Roxeth' by Foy Publications Ltd., E. Molesey, Surrey

TEN SHILLINGS AND SIXPENCE NET

Limited First Edition 1948

Printed in England
by A. W. Duncan & Co. Ltd., Seel Street, Liverpool

Acknowledgments

In compiling this first Miscellany of Roxeth, I have been greatly helped by the researches of the Rev. W. Done Bushell and Sir Montagu Sharpe and by books on the Church, the School and the District by Samuel Gardner, P. Thornton, W. W. Druett, H. S. Braun and Percy Davenport.

The County Librarian has lent 'out of print' books. Miss Cameron has introduced me to interesting records at the Middlesex Guildhall, and helpful officials at the British Museum, the Public Records Office, the National Portrait Gallery, and the Middlesex Land Registry have brought to light and facilitated the reproduction of documents, maps and pictures ; in the text and under the illustrations I have endeavoured to record my indebtedness to authors, artists, photographers and public authorities, but even with the valued help of Mrs. Sherwood, who keeps a register of the 'Friends of Roxeth', I could not hope to list all those who have co-operated in this little venture to put Roxeth back on the map.

For many years I have been helped and encouraged by Mr. Sydney Walton and in co-operation with Mrs. Sherwood, Mr. George Champness and other friends of Roxeth, he is sponsoring this first edition of the Story of Roxeth.

The Rev. J. E. Penney has read the proofs and Foy Publications have overcome production difficulties all along the line. To each and all of these I am indebted.

TOM BARTLETT

91, *Woodend Avenue,*
Roxeth.
8th November, 1945—8th March, 1948.

FOREWORD

A somewhat racy but very apt slogan has been coined and is frequently used by Mr. T. L. Bartlett, the author of this delightful book on " The Story of Roxeth "—" HATS OFF TO THE PAST, COATS OFF TO THE FUTURE." Nothing could summarise better the aim and purpose behind the book and all his interest in " good old Roxey."

He was born and bred in the locality when Roxeth was a peaceful agricultural village nourishing a very real community life and spirit. He has seen the district grow into a vast dormitory suburb of Greater London with nearly all the fields and water meadows (where once he and his friends used to wander watching the birds), covered by houses and criss-crossed by concrete roads until little is left of open space for the children of the present.

More than that, he realised to his horror that the old community spirit was being kept alive only by a very small circle of people. Even the proud and ancient name " Roxeth " was being generally abandoned south of the Piccadilly Railway in favour of the soulless " South Harrow " dictated by the authorities of the same railway.

Before all is entirely lost he has entered the lists in a most praiseworthy endeavour to save the good old name with its wondrous associations and traditions. At the same time he believes, and surely rightly, that if only the inhabitants of Roxeth to-day can learn what a priceless heritage is theirs and regain their pride in it, there will be a revival of a true community spirit to hand down to coming generations.

In furtherance of his aim, he has painstakingly undertaken a full and laborious research into Roxeth's history, the result of which is this little book, albeit enlivened with a certain amount of imaginative insight when actual evidence was lacking. He has also been instrumental in founding a small body of people called " the Friends of Roxeth " who have been able to procure the restoration of the ancient boundary stones (*Frontispiece*).

They have fought hard with him in endeavouring to preserve two ancient monuments of Roxeth—The Old Barn and the Moat. The former, alas, has now been pulled down, but the latter remains surrounded by the remnants of buttercup fields. Naturally it is an ambition of the author that his book will help to stir up further interest to forward the struggle to preserve the Moat as a monument of the past and to retain the fields as an open space for the children of to-day.

Much indeed could be written in commendation of this work in general and this book in particular, but space forbids. I can only say how proud and honoured I am to be asked to write a foreword to the book and that it is my sincere hope that it will receive in full measure the appreciation it deserves so richly and that it may indeed succeed in helping substantially to further the fulfilment of the aims and vision of Mr. T. L. Bartlett and " The Friends."

J. EDWARD PENNEY, *Vicar of St. Paul's*,
Roxeth, Harrow, Middlesex.

CONTENTS

PART I

THE STORY OF ROXETH

PART II

THE SPIRIT OF ROXETH

PART III

THE CHALLENGE OF ROXETH

CHAPTER ONE

ROXETH BEFORE THE CONQUEST

(Frontinus to Leofwine)

MOST of the people who sleep inside the bounds of the ancient and extensive manor of Roxeth call it South Harrow. They know next to nothing of its boundaries, its traditions, its history. To them it is not a heritage but a characterless extension of London's dormitory with the usual complement of shops, buses, a cinema and a station.

The station is blatantly but wrongly named South Harrow. It was therefore an ill day for Roxeth and its good name when a blue enamelled board labelled "South Harrow Station—for Roxeth and Northolt" appeared in the Toll Gate Road. It was followed by another at Headstone "Live at North Harrow—a place of tone." The era of progress, false values and grab had started. The obliteration of beautiful lanes, ancient footpaths, old place names, old boundary stones, old memories and old memorials had begun. Roxeth and Headstone were under a cloud—a thick nasty cloud; but truth has a high survival value. After two centuries the honest English tongue triumphed over the Latinised Norman lisp and I have little doubt that Headstone and Roxeth (good old Roxey!) will one day come into their own again and triumph over North and South Harrow.

Of the thousands who use South Harrow Station few remember what old Roxeth was like. They never knew its fields and lanes, its farms and cottages, its marshes and orchards. They never sat on the white "Postes" where Woolworth stands or went courting down the Long Mile. They did not attend its drag hunts, visit its shooting butts or watch Charles Fleet rising in his balloon over its fields on bank holidays. They did not see the early motors jib at Harrow Hill or follow Dodds coal cart down the Long Mile to pick up the remains of a Wilbur Wright aeroplane that had flown all the way from Wembley Park.

Where the huntsmen assembled they now line up in a cinema queue but they have never processed down Northolt Road with Britannia and the toothless lion or followed Buffalo Bill and his painted redskins into Hall's field as Lord George Sanger led the way to a special afternoon performance. That was before "the Arches" were built! Nor did they listen to the circus announcer proclaiming, " on my right, Gunner O'Neal. On my left (caw ! caw ! caw !) damn those rooks. I shall have to get my gun !" Those rooks were an essential part of old Roxey. From them we get the first part of our ancient good name, HROCES-SEATH. " HROC " is an old Danish word for rook. It links our story not only with Corvus Frugileus, No. 4 Bird on the British Ornithological list but with the Danes—the Canutes and the Hardicanutes who replaced the Watlings and the Gumenings—with the hardy Danes who came foraging up the Thames with rooks carved on the prows of their flat-bottomed boats and rook emblems gleaming on their helmets as they broke through the primeval forest into the Roxeye marshes. By the Treaty of Wedmore 879 the line of Watling Street (the present line of Edgware Road and the L.M.S.) was fixed on parchment as the boundary between the Saxons and the Danes, but the marshes around Roxeth and forests around Harrow must long have been a no-mans land between the contending Saxons and Danes. Names like Roxeth suggest that the Danes continued in possession of some settlements well to the west of Watling Street.

From the very beginning the district appears to have had two names—" HROCES-SEATH " and " HROCS-EYE " the ancient equivalents of Roxeth and Roxey. Other variants of the name with their dates are ROKESHEYE 1205, ROKESEIE 1246, ROXE 1327, ROXHETHE 1422, ROXEHAY 1508, ROXHEY 1550, ROXETH 1710, ROXEY 1745. " Hroc " means a rook, but what sort of a possession of a rook is a " Seath " or " Seadum ?" Seath has been variously interpreted by experts as " the seat," " the abode," " the home," " the spring," " the fount," " the marsh," " the pit," " the well," " the lake " of the rooks. Where pedants differ popular usage sometimes comes to the rescue and there is much less doubt about what " HROCS-EYE " (Good old Roxey !) means. It means the marshy isle of the rooks. In days gone by rivers and streams were rarely cleaned or channelled by human agency so they overflowed into marshes. Before the Thames was embanked it was bordered by marshes and by marshy islands (eyots) at Bermondsey (Bermond-eye), at Westminster (Thorn-eye), at Chelsea (Chels-eye). So the popular name Roxeye tells us not only something about the early inhabitants of this district but something about the nature of the district they inhabited.

Two thousand years ago Roxeth was marshy ground in the midst of a great primeval forest. This forest was infested with wild boar, deer, wolves and other savage beasts. It was crossed by only a few trackways and in all probability the nearest trackway to Roxeth ran northwards past Horsendon and Brockley Hills to the Head Quarters of the fighting Catevellauni near St. Albans. This warlike tribe camped north of the great earthwork known as Grims Dyke which stretches for miles east and west of Harrow Weald leading at each end to an ancient British Park or Wild

Beast Enclosure. Possibly because the Catevellauni leaders kept fit by hunting in their Wild Beast Park at Ruislip this tribe was able to put up a stiffer resistance to the invading Romans than the other tribes.

Two thousand years ago between 25th August and 26th September Julius Ceasar must have passed through or very near to Roxeth. A century later, A.D. 61, somewhere in the neighbourhood of Harrow Weald Common, there was a frightful slaughter of Boadicea's followers. The Roman occupation of Britain lasted for nearly four hundred years. All the time the Romans were making roads and walls, and building their towns complete with baths, temples and theatres. They gave the conquered Britons good laws and a strong government.

Roxeth has something which is even older than its ancient good name—its boundaries. Julius Agricola is known as the Roman propraetor who completed the conquest of Britain. His predecessor, Julius Frontinus, was an exceedingly able administrator. He was also an engineer and a great authority on land surveying. According to Tacitus " an instinct for public improvements dominated his career." During his procuratorship of Britain, A.D. 74—78, the survey and skilful subdivision of the London territorium into four pagi began. The London territorium was the quadrilateral enclosed by the waters of the Thames, the Colne and the Lea.

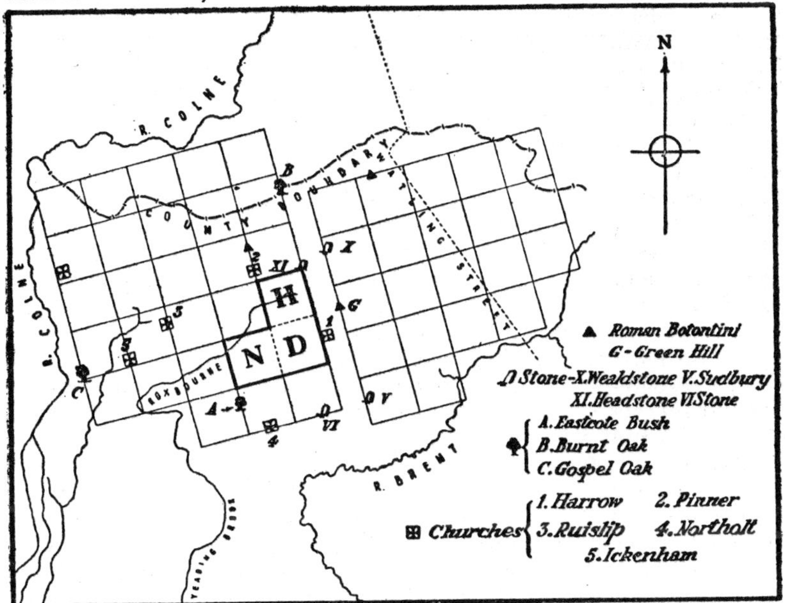

SURVEY LINES which suggest that the 3 Roxeth tything or common field areas date back to Roman times.

Adapted from maps by Sir Montagu Sharpe—Author " Antiquities of Middlesex " Methuen.

Subsequently this area became the county of Middlesex although one half of one of the original Roman pagi was incorporated in Hertfordshire so that the powerful abbot of St. Albans might have all his land in the same county.

The four pagi of the London territorium were each subdivided into fifty square plots, each 1,980 yards long. These squares were called posseda and the position of the three Roman posseda in the North pagus, which later developed into the three Roxeth tythings Newton, Dobbs and Heath, can still be indicated by geometric lines printed across a map and confirmed by lines of elms which still delineate the western boundary of Roxeth.

The Romans were clever local administrators; for, having set up their own boundary, measuring and memorial stones, they tactfully restored ancient local shrines. Then in the month of May, at the Ambarvalia, the Magister Pagi or other local government official arranged processions to, and celebrations at, the shrines, and lustrations or beatings at the boundary stones where TERMINUS (who was a Roman god before he became an English railway station) was honoured with garlands as the protector of boundaries. These ceremonies at the boundary stones and shrines helped to make the local residents proud of their pagus, and made them conscious of how and where their posseda differed from others. It was thus that the ancient practice of "beating the bounds" began. It was continued by the mediaeval church and has survived in many parishes, including Roxeth, Stanmore and Northolt, to the present time.

A good deal can be learned about our ancient history from surviving place names and from others which appear on old maps. Names like the Hundred of Gore (Spears), Bonefield X, between Roxeth and Eastcote, and Haest (fierce conflict) Hill X, indicate that there was bitter fighting in the neighbourhood before its land was finally parcelled into Shires, Hundreds, vils and manors; and Roxeth became a subsidiary manor in the great ecclesiastical Harrow manor in the Hundred of Gore in the County of Middlesex. The earliest mention in writing of Middlesex (Middleseaxan) is 704, of Harrow (Hergae) 767 and of Roxeth (Hroces-seath) 845.

The arrangement of the ancient lanes and trackways leading up to, round, and out of the old village of HROCS-EYE (Rooks marsh) furnishes a clue to its forgotten history. Three roads (formerly known as Lower Roxeth Road, Middle Roxeth Road, and London Hill) unite and point in arrow head formation at the site of Roxeth's moated Grange. To the south of this at Eastcroft Lane (now almost obliterated by the Gas Works) the old roads bulged outward to enclose an oval shaped area. Similiar ovals were enclosed by old roads at Pinner and Ruislip and they take us back to the days when it was necesary to surround the inner core of the hamlet with earthworks and stockades. At Ruislip parts of the ancient defences remain, and at Roxeth, before St. Margarets Avenue replaced the crescent shaped rookery, the southern edge of enclosed village could be traced on foot or seen as a whole from the neighbouring Viaduct. Ancient trackways led southward and eastward from the stockaded village across the marshes. One, known as Dobbs Mill Lane, led past Northalla (Northolt) towards the Archbishop's other manor at Hesa (Hayes). The other led in three right angle bends north westward towards the stockaded village of Pinner. A third Roman straight path (The Long Mile) separated Newton Field from Dobbs Field.

Other clues to our story are to be found in the composition of the soil, the general lay of the land (before houses obstructed vision) and from remains varying in size from old coins and flint arrowheads to Grange Moat and Grims Dyke. In my garden there is a piece of the Sarsen stone on which gipsy kings were crowned. It was rescued from Woodend Lane in 1929 when the steam roller was at work. Other records of the past were brought to light when two new railways were cut through Roxeth at the beginning of the century.

Apart from geological and archaeological evidence, there are four ancient parchments which carry our story back three hundred years before the Doomsday Book.

1. THE GRANT BY OFFA A.D. 767. This Canterbury parchment contains the oldest known reference to Harrow. It states "I Offa King of the Mercians freely grant to Stidbert the Abbot thirty hides of land in Middlesex between the Harrow of the Gumenings and the Lidding and there are six hides and a dwelling house on the Eastern bank of the Lidding brook and Stidbert has by way of exchange transferred to me thirty hides of land in Chiltern." The document concludes with a warning to those who tamper with ancient endowments—" and if any man, as may it never happen, essay to meddle wrongfully with this exchange of ours let him be well aware that he shall answer for it before Christ and his angels." It was witnessed by Archbishop Jaenbert.

As Mr. Hugh Braun has located Stidberts land and the Lidding Brook in Kenton and as Mr. Druett has located it in Pinner, I venture to suggest that Roxeth Grange is the oldest recorded dwelling site in the Harrow district and that Roxeth's ancient brook, The Roxbourne, is the stream described in the 767 Charter. This brook rises in the south western corner of the School cricket fields and after flowing between Roxeth and Pinner and between Eastcote and Northolt it becomes, near Downe Barn, the Yedding Brook. Did the hitherto unlocated area of Herefrethingland (common land) lie along this brook and did it near Prior's Field, link up Werhards two Christ Church establishments at Harrow and Hayes? Greenford and Hayes, (not Kenton and Pinner) are the places which appear to be linked to Harrow through Christ Church Canterbury in the early charters. Wherever Harrow of the Gumenings—and Lidding is located—there remains an endorsement on the back of this charter stating that Earl Pilheard secured possession of this land and house at the Witenagemot held at Chelsea in 801. So I like to think of him as the second known proprietor of Roxeth Grange.

2. THE COUNCIL OF CLOVESHO A.D. 825 parchment was witnessed by Cwoenthryth daughter of Cenwulf, by Beonwulf King of Mercia, Wulfred Archbishop of Canterbury, Wilred Bishop elect of Dunwich and many other distinguished clerics and nobles. In this lengthy document lands and manors belonging to the Mercian royalty were conveyed to Archbishop Wulfred, and so the eight century long connection between Harrow, Roxeth, Yedding, and Canterbury began.

This historic conveyance of the Harrow Manor lands is commemorated by a window in Harrow Church. It is there called a 'restoration' and Cwoenthyrth—the reputed murderer of her little brother Saint Kenelm, has been whitewashed and looks quite holy as the suppliant abbess of Southminster.

3. THE WILL OF WERHARD A.D. 832 details the lands 100 hides and four hides held at Harrow, Wembley Yeading and Herefrethingland by Werhard priest of Christ Church Canterbury. It bequeaths to 5 poor people at Harrow twenty six pence each for clothing and as much food as may reasonably appear sufficient to their needs. It requests that daily masses for Wulfred and all those who befriend Christ Church should be said; and it decrees that on Wulfreds' Anniversarium 1200 loaves with cheese or bacon fat be given to the poor.

In his Octocentenary Tract about "Wulfred and Cwoenthryth" the Rev. W. Done Bushell writes "I hope those 5 people are still fed and clothed; I hope the daily mass is duly said at Harrow or at Roxeth and if so that the Vicar does not fail to pray for Werhard the priest and abbot. I mention Roxeth as well as Harrow for you will observe that Werhard had to do not only with Harrow but with Roxeth also"

4. THE HROCES SEATH PARCHMENT is dated Sunday, 8th November, A.D. 845 and as it relates specifically to Roxeth, the ancient abode of Rooks, the Rev. Done Bushell's translation of the document is given in full.

Exchange of Land at Roxeth,
8th November, 845.

"The lord our God, the Lord of Hosts being King for ever this exchange of land, that is of two hides is hereby made between Werhard the Priest and Abbot and Werenberht, servant of the King and Thegn for the common convenience of us both, that is to say I, Werenberht the Thane do of my own free will convey to Werhard the Abbot one hide of land of my own private property in exchange for other like land which also lies within the limits of the district which is by the inhabitants called ROXETH with the fields and woods and meadows and all rights duly and lawfully belonging to the same, which land did aforetime appertain to the well known place called Greenford, for him to have and to hold and without let or hindrance to enjoy in perpetuity with the same free tenure with which also aforetime . . .

Done in the year of the Incarnation of our Lord 845 being the 8th of the Indiction on Sunday, the 8th Day of November at the City of London those witnesses whose names are written at the foot of this Charter being present and giving their confirmation with the sign of the Holy Cross of Christ.

I, Ceolnoth by grace of God Archbishop confirm the exchange of land and subscribe thereunto with the sign of the Holy Cross of Christ.

I, Turnberht Bishop agree and subscribe (Then follow the names of 8 other Bishops, Ceolred, Berehtred, Alchhun, Hunberht, Willred, Coelberht, Gutheard, Tatnoth).

I, Werhard Abbot agree and subscribe.

I, Werenberht agree and subscribe."

The five words—thane, abbot, fields, woods, meadows, suggest that in 845 Roxeth was almost a model Saxon village. Possibly its buildings included a group of wooden cottages, a small new monastery for the monks whom Werhard reinstated in 830, a big barn, and the ancestral house of the Thane who held Roxeth for and in the King's name. Close to the cottages there would be small " yards " or enclosures for feeding stock and beyond these Roxeth's three unhedged fields (two to the South and one to the North) divided in long strip allotments, separated only by grass verges, and shared out amongst the families so that each cultivator knew exactly which strips he must cultivate and which leave fallow in any particular year. Documents such as that in the Middlesex Land Register 1765, Vol. 1, No. 591, and maps such as Roques 1745 show that this communal open field system of cultivation continued in Roxeth and other parts of Middlesex right down to the eighteenth century.

The changing landlords who owned Roxeth down the ages claimed changing rights of service from the villagers. Their tenants were tied to the land but whether they were ploughmen, bee-keepers, pig stewards, haymakers or pounders they had certain common rights of pasturage and pannage and as Roxeth was for many centuries very rich, both in commonland and woodland, this may have helped to breed an independent type of labourer who believed in the ancient rights of good old Roxey.

Abbot Werhard, presbyter and 'prepotens in Anglia' was related to Archbishop Wulfred. He owned land at Harrow, Heyes, Roxeth, Greenford, Otford and other places and his name appears on many ancient charters and documents as well as in the Anglo-Saxon Chronicle of A.D. 850. He resided at Heyes and his Will seems to imply a cell or settlement of Christ Church monks in this neighbourhood. The special hide he obtained from Werenberht may have been his special gift to his Christ Church brothers in Roxeth as a centre for their work and the place where masses could be said for Archbishop Wulfred.

I have been unable to trace the further story of Werenberht and his sons in the fights that ensued before King Alfred forced the Danes back first across Watling Street and then across the River Lee.

Ceolberht, Bishop of London succeeded Ceolnoth as Archbishop of Canterbury but owing to the Danish disturbances neither appears to have been enthroned at Canterbury. (A coin of Ceolberht is preserved in the London Guildhall Museum). The big assembly of Wessex and Mercian bishops who were unitedly present when the Roxeth parchment was attested may be in part due to some of them being evacuees from sees that had been plundered by the Danes. The sees of all these witnessing bishops have been traced, one of them, Dunwich, to the bottom of the English Channel.

*For a fuller representation of the Roxeth parchment in time and space see Chapter Six—" The Thane of Roxey."

DEATH OF LEOFWINE, brother of King Harold, as depicted on the Bayeux tapestry.

CHAPTER TWO

THE PASSING OF THE NORMANS

(Lanfranc to Chaucer)

JUST before the Norman Conquest Roxeth was included in the earldom of Leofwine, the brother of King Harold. This Saxon warrior is pictured on the Bayeux Tapestry. He died fighting at Hastings and his lands at Harrow passed to Lanfranc the new Norman Archbishop. " In the hundred of Gore Archbishop Lanfranc holds Harrow." Lanfranc's hundred hides incorporated Roxeth, Headstone, Sudbury, Pinner, Wembley and other subsidiary manors and hamlets—a girdle round the Hill.

Herges was then the largest vil or manor in Middlesex. It was slightly bigger than the present Harrow Urban District Council area (12,558 acres) and it ranked as the fourth richest Middlesex manor though its registered population of one priest, three knights, vassals, villanes and cottagers could hardly have numbered more than six hundred souls.

Benedictine monks from Lanfranc's Abbey of Bec (which came into the news again on D. Day) followed quickly in the train of William and his Norman Knights and they at once set to work scheduling, taking over and improving church owned lands. At the time of the Conquest nearly half Middlesex was owned by the Church. New churches to carry on the tradition of Bec were built at Harrow, Ruislip and St. Albans. Brooks were channelled, marshes drained, mills, manors, barns and dovecotes built. Then in accordance with the Doomsday recommendation " At Herges there are 45 ploughs in use and there could be 16 more " good Roxeth earth was rescued from alder swamps and the production of food for man and hay for his horses was increased.

But the new Norman administrators of Roxeth did not spend all their time hedging and ditching and building. Long strip common field cultivation was continued by vassals under clerical supervision and some at least of the owners found time for hunting, hawking and fishing. The Archbishop's lands between the hilltop and Northolt were well stocked with game as is evidenced by the following short but very interesting Royal Charter of 1070.

> " King William to Geoffrey Sheriff and all other his faithful citixens of London sendeth greeting . . .
>
> I hereby order and admonish you that on the lands of

Lanfranc the Archbishop which belong to his Manor of Harrow ye chase neither stags nor hinds nor fallow deer nor hunt at all on them except so far as he may order and permit."

As this Geoffrey de Mandeville, Port Reeve of London and Lord of the Manor of Northolt also held two hides somewhere in the Archbishop's area (possibly Mount Park) it is easy to picture him and his faithful Londoners spending a week-end away from the London docks chasing a fine fat buck up hill and down dale all the way from Northolt past Woodend to Mount Pleasant and Roxey Corner.

What did Mount Pleasant, Roxeth and the Moated Grange look like in those days? How much water for horse washing was there in the pond and how much mead and venison at the Grange? Were spoonbill marshes being drained for cultivation and were oak trees which provided Gurths two thousand hogs (ii mille porcis) with food being felled to provide timber for a new Norman church on the Hill? This church of which little but the western doorway remains, was built by Lanfranc but it was not consecrated until a second Archbishop from Bec—the saintly Anselm—had succeeded to the See of Canterbury and the manors of Harrow.

" Dark was the forest, heron haunted the marshes,
The rooks of old Roxeth were cawing their loudest
When the mason from Bec awoke from his slumbers.
' Curse that great Saxon what a noise he is making
Felling that oak tree. He is worse than the rooks.'
' Speak not so harshly,' said Anslem the gentle
' Although he seems witless look at his muscles
We want simple strength in the church we are building
It needs a brave mixture to make a good world '."

Lanfranc, who was one of the principal landowners of Middlesex died in 1087 ; but the office of Archbishop was not filled till 1093. In the meantime the Crown appropriated the revenues of the Archbishop's lands at Harrow. Ranolf Flambard was financial adviser to William Rufus when this happened, so it seems likely that the connection of the Flambard family with Harrow may date from the beginning of the long drawn out quarrel between the Kings of England and the Archbishops of Canterbury. In these quarrels the Archbishop's lands and manors on and around the Hill were frequently involved.

It is correct to speak of the Harrow Manors in the plural for the Archbishop's twelve thousand acres embraced at different times a Rectory Manor and Manor House on the hilltop, and several other manors or sub-manors—Notably those of Roxeth, Sudbury, Headstone, Woodall and Uxendon. How large the great Manor of Roxeth was can be judged from surviving references of its transfers between 1371 (when it passed from Archbishop Whittesley to

(*Photo by* F. White)

The Ancient Moat and Great Barn at Roxeth Grange

(*By permission of the* British Museum

The Roxeth Charter of a.d. 845

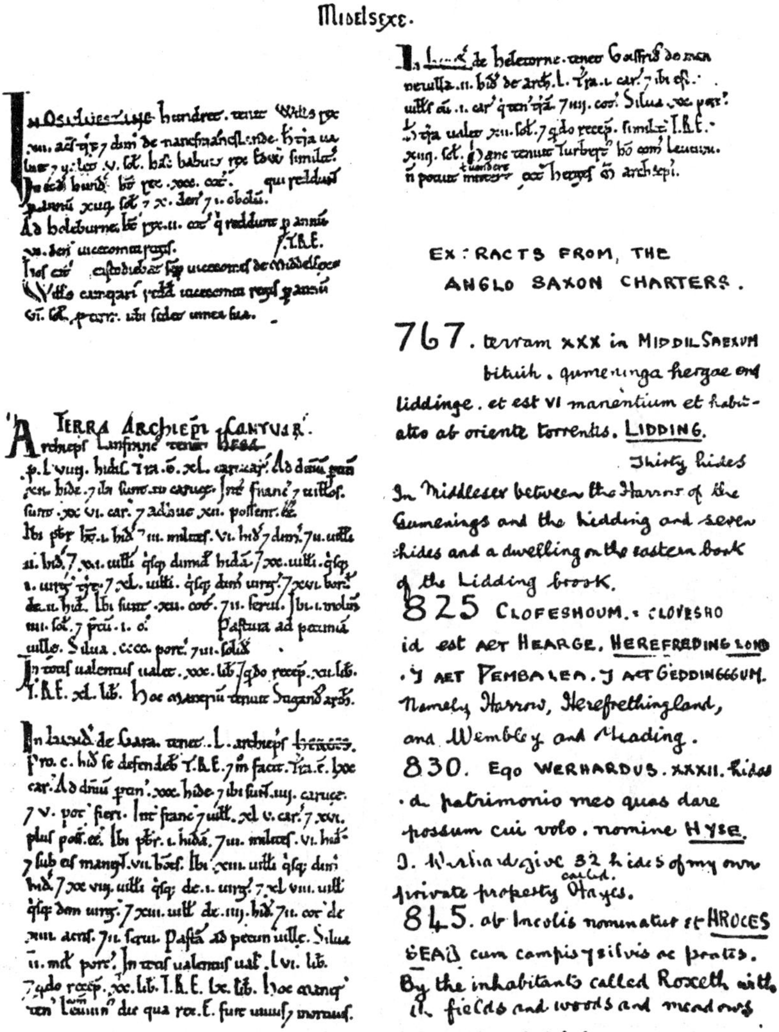

DOMESDAY BOOK ENTRY of lands held by Lanfranc Leofwine, Mandeville and Flambard.
(Inset transcription and translation of extracts from four SAXON CHARTERS).

Sir Nicholas Brembre) and 1764 (when it passed from Brian Taylor to Percival Hart).

One of the unsolved mysteries of local history is where the Saxon and early Norman Archbishops Lanfranc, Anselm, Theobald, and Becket lived when they came to Harrow. Was it in the Rector's Manor in the Grove to the north of the Church or did they have a manor house of their own? Did they have a landlord's interest in one hundred and four hides at Harrow and a resident interest in one particular hide at Roxeth? Did Werhard establish a church house at Roxeth as well as one at Hayes? Claims have been advanced that the Archbishops put up at either Headstone or Sudbury. This may be true for the later Plantagenet Archbishops, but not for the early Norman ones. The tradition, dating from the Harrow Pageant, that Becket as well as Wolsey put up at Headstone is almost certainly wrong, for the date of the acquisition of Headstone Manor by the Archbishops is 1344.

It appears more likely that the Norman Archbishops put up at Roxeth for :—

1. Roxeth's direct connections with Canterbury go back farther than those of Headstone. Possibly to Stidbert and Jaenbert and certainly to Werhard and Wulfred.
2. Therefore I suggest that Werhard reinstated the dispossessed monks at Roxeth in 830 and that the rich hide of Roxeth land he obtained from Weremberht was a gift to this foundation.
3. This rich arable land, midway between the oak clad hilltop and the undrained marshes, conveyed with such ample ceremonial on 8th November, 845 to the church may be identical with the priest's hide scheduled in the Doomsday survey of 1086.
4. As the local residence of the Archbishops is repeatedly called a Grange, the place at which Becket met Theobald, entertained the papal Emissaries and welcomed Abbot Simon at the gate may have been Roxeth Grange.
5. The antiquity of Roxeth Grange is proved by the presence of a very ancient moat which has been scheduled by H.M. Commissioners as one of the four Historic Monuments of the Harrow district.
6. Tradition associates this moat with King Stephen, and the Great Barn which overlooks it with John Wesley.
7. Roxeth Grange is nearer the church on the hilltop than either Headstone or Sudbury. The distance from Harrow spire to Roxeth Moat is 1150 yards, and the convergence of many routes at Roxeth Grange helps to confirm that it has long been a place of importance.

A tradition which cannot be ignored associates the Grange Roxeth with King Stephen (King Stephen's Moat) and in a letter dated 28th October, 1945, Mr. Walter W. Druett, author of "Harrow down the Ages" wrote: "I did intend one day to search out the story of Roxeth but ill health and the war years have made this impossible. There is one legend which I always thought most interesting. I was told years ago that one of the old chroniclers stated that King Stephen who became king after Henry in 1135 and whose twenty years' reign were years of misrule and disorder—lived at Roxeth. This is quite possible as there was much unrest in London over the rival claims of Matilda and Stephen."

With Geoffery de Mandeville, Lord of the Manor of Northolt and Constable of The Tower of London, constantly changing sides and offering The Tower to the highest bidder, Stephen may sometimes have felt himself safer at Roxeth than inside the Tower.

In 1143 when the anarchy of Stephen's reign had lasted for eight years a young man put up at one of our local inns. His hostess dreamed that she saw this young man squatting on the roof of Harrow Church and that his robes covered the whole edifice. Harrow Church was then without a steeple. The strong young man with exceptionally good eyesight and hearing was Thomas Becket then known as TOME LUND—Thomas of London.

He had come, in the prime of his life to the Court of Archbishop Theobald at Harrow to offer his service to a powerful church which was becoming more powerful. Although he quarrelled with another young man who was to become the future Archbishop of York his rise to power was rapid. He served Henry II faithfully as Chancellor of England but when that monarch elevated him to the Archbishopric of Canterbury the historic struggle between Henry II and Becket began. It was a struggle that shook Christendom.

In 1163 Thomas the Archbishop held his court—possibly at Roxeth Grange, and there entertained the papal emissaries—(an abbot, a count and a bishop.) They persuaded him against his better judgement to submit at Clarendon to Henry's claims over the church. Between such a King and such an Archbishop there could be no lasting reconciliation and for six years Becket was an exile at Pontigny. Then he returned to his own country, his own cathedral and his own manor at Harrow. Simon Abbot of St. Albans (as illustrated on one of the windows of Harrow Church) failed to effect a reconciliation between the Archbishop and the King. I have always pictured Matthew Paris' account of the last residence of St. Thomas at Harrow (from 12th to 17th December, 1170. He was martyred on 29th December) as centering around Roxeth's moated Grange, but until the site of our great archbishop's house is proved by manuscripts and excavation I have thought best to continue the story of St. Thomas as one of the memories of St. Edmund's Pond. (Chapter 7).

After quarrelling with Archbishop Stephen Langton, King John retained possession of Harrow and kept ten greyhounds there. He may have raced hares across Roxeth Common before turning south to hawk over the Roxeye marshes or north to hunt in the great forest which was still full of wild beasts. There seems little doubt that in the 13th Century Roxeth was a happy hunting ground for Kings, Sherriffs, Bishops and Constables of the Tower.

In 1205 the lands of Ralph de Roxesheye (Roxeth) were transferred to Roger de la Dunne, Constable's of the Tower. As in the well witnessed transfer of A.D. 845 an archbishop (Hubert Fitzwalter), the proud City of London, and a famous cleric (Elias de Derham) again figure prominently in this transfer of Roxeth lands.

The Tower was held for the King and when the Ceremony of the Keys was being performed, yeomen throats slaked with barley mow from the Constable's Roxey harvest fields may have shouted, "Vive le Roi Edouard!" "Vive le Roi Henri!" "God bless King Richard!" We cannot fix the night on which the challenge words changed from Norman–French back to honest English, but during the two centuries which followed the Battle of Hastings, the English speaking folk were slowly reasserting themselves.

During the long reign of Henry III 1206—1272, Harrow Church was rebuilt with a spire and furnished with an endowment. Elias de Derham, Rector of Harrow and architect of Salisbury Cathedral, played a part in the rebuilding ,and the endowment was arranged by Archbishop (later Saint) Edmund de Pontigny. This endowment included not only the parishioners' tithes of land, cheese, chickens, little pigs, goats and bees, but the great tithe of the hay of Hamo and Hugh de Rokesie and their successors. Hamo de Rokesie was one of the signatories of the Harrow Church endowment and I like to think of him as the occupant of Roxeth's Tythe Farm. If his hay grew in Newton's Field and Hugh's in Dobbs Field this may explain why Roxeth's Tithe Barn was built on the boundary road between these two tythings. Tithe farm survives but the old bench marked Tithe Barn has been replaced by an up-to-date Public House. Farmer Priest the last haymaking yeoman of Newton Field was, like Hamo, a good churchman. He was laid to rest in Roxeth church-yard forty years ago.

The pond at Roxeth Corner, which was known for centuries as St. Edmund's Pond, must have witnessed many interesting episodes in the story of Roxeth and the name may well be another interesting link between Roxeth and Saint Edmund Rich the Archbishop who endowed Harrow Church. It is referred to in 1850 as a mucky horsepond but as it was only 200 yards from Roxeth's Moated Grange it may once have been a neat well stocked fish pond inside an Archbishop's garden.

Archbishop Boniface, uncle of Queen Eleanor, succeeded saintly Edmund Rich as Lord of the Manor. He seems to have been as tough as the times in which he lived, for when the prior of St. Bartholomew objected to his visitation he flattened the Prior out with his fist and then fled from the wrath of London to the Manor which had sheltered King Stephen and St. Thomas the Martyr. Finding the Harrow folk not averse to his visitation he obtained for them a weekly market and a three day fair at the Feast of the Nativity of the Blessed Virgin Mary.

For over six hundred years (1262—1872) the Harrow fairs continued, and as they often stretched from Middle Roxeth Road to the Church fields along the edge of the Harrow desmesne lands, they gave movement and colour to the Roxeth side of the Hill. To add to the fun of the fair and to provide a diversion from compulsory archery a pair of stocks, two horseponds and a special court (Pie Poudre) were available for dealing with market sharpers and other offenders.

Edward I visited Harrow six times. Most of these visits were in the spring, and he probably enjoyed them ; for though the area under cultivation was increasing there were still plenty of woods, wastes, and Heron marshes and few hedges to obstruct the passage or the vision of the Royal hawking parties. Edward I was particularly fond of hawking, and on 12th May, 1305, after inspecting the Archery Butts he may have proceeded, pennants flying, down through the greenery of Roxeth Hill to spend three days at the Archbishop's grange, hawking in the Roxeye marshes and visiting the adjoining hamlet of Greenford. The last time Edward I came to Harrow he was accompanied by a mighty army in battle array for he was on his way to hammer the Scots. How efficiently and uncomfortably his knights were dressed can be guessed from the brass effigy of Sir Edmund Flambard in Harrow Church. By way of contrast to the knight's pointed helmet, chain mail necklet and armour covered by a sleeveless coat, Lady Elizabeth Flambard whose memorial brass has been missing for 150 years, wore a smart gown, a flowing mantle and a headdress decorated with wavy lines. She carried a pomander or scent box and she was followed by a faithful hound. The illustration which shows the missing brass of the Lady Elizabeth has been copied for me from Groses "Antiquities", by Malcom Norris.

From old Church brasses, from Harrow Manor Court rolls, from Langlands "Vision of Piers Ploughman," and from Chaucers "Canterbury Tales" we can make a panorama of the fine folk who attended the rich ceremonial services in St. Mary's Church, the stewards and the tything men who presided and witnessed at the Manor Courts, and the forgotten folk who worked in the frost or the broiling sun in Newton Field or queued at Dobbs Mill for their corn to be ground.

Most of them were tied to the soil which maintained them. Unlike their suburban successors they knew the place to which they belonged ; some who travelled far with their lords to London Town, Picardie and Jerusalem carried memories of long furrows of sprouting Roxeth corn with them and wished themselves back in their dark cottages by the rook swamp. Often these hard working ignorant peasants were cruelly treated, and maybe some of Roxeth's

Brass of Sir Edmund Flambard, c. 1370. The brass figure of the Lady Elizabeth, missing from the chancel floor of St. Mary's Church, is shewn.

haymakers demonstrated round the Grange moat before marching with the men of St. Albans to London to demand the head of Archbishop Sudbury, their landlord. He was sheltering in the Tower but this did not save his head from the axe. It was then trundled round complete with Mitre, and fixed on London Bridge to be exchanged later for the head of Wat Tyler when the peasants were again under control . . . and while a new archbishop was being found Richard II became landlord of Harrow.

It is within the bounds of possibility that about this time Geoffrey Chaucer visited Roxeth Grange and Northolt Church. He had as his colleague at the Customs Office, a distinguished and hospitable Londoner who was destined to open a new chapter in the story of Roxeth ; and maybe this first Lord of the independent Manor of Roxeth invited his friend the poet to ride out to Roxeth's moated Grange, to meet the Lady Idonea and her masterful children.

Arms of
Sir Nicholas Brembre
Lord Mayor
from font in Northolt Church

Arms of
Geoffrey Chaucer
from his tomb in the Abbey

CHAPTER THREE

ROXETH MANOR

(From Brembre to Dudley)

OUTLAWS and conspirators loom large in local and national histories. I was therefore not surprised to see a statement in Harrow's local paper that Roxeth was named after a very famous outlaw called William Roxeth. Actually this William was a rich landowner and like the Harwes of Harwe he was entitled to the name Roxheth of Roxheth. Towards the end of the reign of Edward III his name appears with increasing frequency in the Manor Court Rolls, and in 1371 William Roxeth of Roxeth became William the Outlaw. His estates were confiscated, and then granted by William Whittesley, Archbishop of Canterbury to Nicholas Brembre, the Lady Idonea, and their heirs as an independent manor. At that time they consisted of a hundred and forty acres. In 845 this area was called a 'cassate'; in Lanfranc's time it was called a "hide," The Roxeth manor also included twelve acres of woodland, five shillings in rents, four cocks valued at sixpence and forty hens valued at three shillings.

This Nicholas Brembre who became Lord of the Manor of Roxeth was something more than London's Leading Grocer (engrosser or wholesaler). He was four times Lord Mayor of London and famous as the man who stood by Richard II "to the death" in the fight against the Lords Appellant. He marches out of the pages of Froissart into our national story, just as Wat Tyler is dying, 'bringing with him a large force on foot' and for his part in that great day's proceedings he was knighted under the Royal Standard, and given a farm worth £40 per annum to add to his manors of Roxeth, Uxendon, Downes and Northolt.

Nicholas Brembre was born in Kent in 1322, a younger son of Sir John Brembre, and being of a fearless nature we find him in the forefront of the economic, social and political upheavals which characterised the reign of Richard II. Like Whittington he was attracted to London. There he sided with Bishop Courtenay and the powerful victualling guilds against the Duke of Lancaster and the poorer non-victualling guilds, who accepted John of Northampton as their trade union organiser and champion. In 1377 just before Edward III died, the Duke of Lancaster was incensed against the Londoners. He deposed Adam Staples, the

Lord Mayor, and Brembre was the strong man appointed to take Adam Staples' place. Nicholas Brembre was a success as Mayor. He pleased his friends by attacking all foreign traders and appeased his enemies by limiting the activities of some multiple traders. He worked for many years with Geoffrey Chaucer at the Customs Office, and was one of the citizens who did not panic when London was overrun by Wat Tyler's men. After witnessing the violent deaths of Treasurer Hales, Archbishop Sudbury and Wat Tyler, he swore to stand by the young King to the death ; and he set about forming a King's party in the City to counteract the activities of Lancaster and John of Northampton.

In 1383 he was elected Lord Mayor and he increased the popularity of the King's party by issuing, on 11th September, 1383 a Proclamation " concerning the liberties lately granted to the citizens of London by the Lord King in his Parliament, and also concerning ancient liberties renewed." He obtained Royal and parliamentary assent to this statement partly by the good offices of the Queen and partly by a gift or loan of 4,000 marks.

How he was the first man to be Lord Mayor in two successive years is told by his enemies in an interesting document which is preserved at the British Museum.

> " Also this year Sir. Nicholl Brember was chosen Maire agene be the saide craftes and by men of the contre at Harrow and the contre there aboughte and not be free eleccion of the citee of London as it owith to be ; and the old halle was stuffed with men at armes be ordinaunce and assente of Sir. Nicholl Brembre fur to choose hym maire on the morrowe : and so it was."

He was elected Mayor for the third year in succession and for the fourth and last time in 1384.

Whilst the Duke of Lancaster was away laying claim to the throne of Castile, opposition to King Richards personal government was concentrated in the hands of the Duke of Gloucester. Gloucester was accordingly invited to supper and assassination at Brembre's house, but failed to turn up and both parties began to prepare for battle. The Lords Appellant mustered forty thousand men at Harringay and asked the King to weed out those traitors, De Vere, de la Pole, Tressilion and Brembre. Sir Nicholas Brembre and Sir Thomas Trivet retaliated by concealing a thousand armed men from their manors in the mews at Charing Cross, with a view to picking off the most obnoxious of the King's uncles as they passed from London to Westminster. Richard would not make war against the Lords Appellant, and though Brembre moved backward and forward from the west to the Tower and then to Wales, he was eventually captured. For a while it was difficult to find a London jury to try the Mayor and King's favourite, but 39 charges were trumpted up against him and he was arraigned in St. Stephen's Hall. He replied to the charges by flinging down his gauntlet and claiming his Knights privilege of trial by combat. This was declined : he was then sentenced to death and after being dragged on a hurdle all the way from Tower Hill, stopping at each furlong for confessions, he was hanged on 20th February, 1388 at Tyburn. He was buried in the great church of Christ Church, Newgate. His arms were emblazoned at the Hall of the Grocers Company and they can still be seen on the ancient font in Northolt Church. A plaque to his memory is also being set up by the "Friends of Roxeth" on the largest of the boundary oaks in Roxeth Recreation Ground.

There are several references to him and his Manors in the Harrow Court Rolls, and in one of these there is a charge that he did not cleanse certain ditches on his land at Roxethe. This was a serious offence in a country which was just recovering from the Black Death but it is one which figures in the court rolls in each century. In 1849 when a special enquiry was held at the Kings Head, drains became a determining factor in the changing story of Roxeth.

In Patent Roll 12 of Richard II dated 1389 the sale of goods and chattels found on the manors of the late Sir Nichols Brembre at Downes, Roxeth, and Northolt is announced. The Roxeth list is particularly interesting because it gives current market prices for Roxeth produce and shows how the Vicarage was linked up with the Roxeth Manor.

"10 quarters of wheat 33/4d.
10 quarters of oats 15/-
20 quarters of peas and beans 40/-
3 cartloads of hay 12/-
1 boar, 1 sow and 2 pigs 6/2d
1 gander and 2 geese 12d.
1 decayed cart for wood and another for dung 4/-
1 bull and 24 cows in the hands of Thomas Godlak £8 6 8d.
11 oxen at Harrow £6 1s. 0d.
3 horses at 30/-
harness for a plough 4/-
7 pigs lately found 2/-
40 acres of land sowed with wheat £6 13s. 4d.
Money owed to the aforesaid Nicholas Brembre by the Vicar of Harrow amounting to 78/4d. which same goods being at Roxeth extend to a value of £33 6s. 2d."

In spite of this notice of sale the Lady Idonea petitioned (it is believed successfully) against the confiscation of her husband's property and there is some uncertainty as to when Roxeth manor, chickens and dung cart returned to the overlordship of Canterbury. Archbishop Thomas Arundel became involved in the quarrels which brought about the downfall of the Plantagenets and he was banished. At the turn of the century notes were made of the claymes of the libtryes of Harrow" "and following a Royal Inspeximus on 14th October, 1399 an Inquisition of the banished Archbishop's castles, lordships and other estates was made. It is in this document, preserved at the Public Record Office, that we again have mention of the Archbishop's Chapel. This with its Grange may have been inside or near the Roxeth Moat, or as Rev. W. Done Bushell suggests, at Sudbury.

In the Middle Ages the State did not function much as a whole, and individuals had few " rights," but because everybody belonged to something—a manor, a monastery, a guild or a borough, corporate action was possible. Local government is not something that Parliament gave England, for Parliament arose out of local government. The Rector of Harrow taking every tenth cock of Roxeth hay from Newton field, or Nicholas Brembre bringing with him a hundred London guildsmen on foot or concealing a thousand retainers (from Roxeth, Downes, Northolt and Uxendon) in the Charing Cross Mews for a special job, are good illustrations of mediæval Corporate action.

Yet even in the days when Lords of the Manor and Abbots were the real powers in the land there were local government representatives. Tythes were made compulsory in the Anglo-Saxon Period but the tything men of the Middle ages were concerned with much more than the collection of the Great Tithe for the Rector. Like the Roman decurio the mediæval tything man was a local government representative. Justice was dispensed and authority for local administration emanated from the Manor. In 1375 Archbishop Simon Sudbury was Lord of Harrow Manor, John de Bukyngham was Lord of Harrow Rectory Manor and Sir Nicholas Brembre was Lord of the Manor of Roxeth. As two of these three were executed and other holders of these offices were often banished, relationship between the parts which made up the Harrow mediæval community, were constantly changing. Yet in the midst of civil wars executions, excommunications and banishings the Harrow Manorial Court Baron and Court Leet continued its work.

The written proceedings of these Courts are preserved in the Middlesex Guild Hall in the famous series of Harrow Manor Court Rolls. They begin in the reign of Edward II, centuries before the Harrow Church Registers, and continue well on into the eighteenth century. The early ones are parchment rolls about one foot wide inscribed in abbreviated Latin, and the entries were apparently taken down at, or very soon after, the cases to which they refer. These courts not only dealt with the Roxeth ponds, ditches, drains, roads, commons and shooting butts, but with the life and conduct of its inhabitants. The Roxeth tything men were continually presenting malefactors, and many interesting sidelights on our changing local story are to be found in these rolls.

The size and importance of the various sub-manors and hamlets which made up the mediæval Harrow community, can be assessed by the number of tything men each sent to the Manor Court· Roxeth usually sent three. Wembley one. In 1424 Roxeth ranked second only to Pinner in the Harrow community.

There is an interesting record of the three Roxeth tything men applying for exemption from their civic duties. They were excused them on payment of fines of 3d., 4d. and 2d. respectively

I am hoping that Mr. Percy Davenport, of Stanmore, will some day publish the story of his researches into the Harrow Manor Court Rolls. Till then the following extracts may serve to carry the story of Roxeth forward a couple of centuries from Brembre to Cranmer.

1384 John Intowne in trouble for sending his son away from Harrow to learn the liberal arts (Harrow has always been conservative).

1392 Reference is made to Les Buttes (the shooting butts) in Roxeth. (In the Manor map of 1759 these butts are shown in the south east corner of Roxeth Common. In the grounds of the house now called "The Moat" and not in the grounds of the house now called "The Butts").

1425 John Roxeth presented for being a common eavesdroppere listening to and prying by night into the secrets of his neighbours to the common nuisance. (Harrow now has a 'Kindly eavesdropper.' He is a friend of Roxeth and good are his reportings).

1443 Presentment that John Webbe, a leper, is dwelling in the Lordship to the common nuisance. The whole tything commended to provide for his removal to Le Lokehouse.

Harrow through Toc H has raised over £1,000 for the relief of lepers in the British Empire—B.E.L.R.A.

1456 John Lyon admitted to lands at Roxeth surrendered by John Greenehill. (These names appear for five centuries in Roxeth and Preston land transfers).

1462 Joan Sextane of Roxeye presented and fined 2d. for refusing to expose her alesign called "Le Alehoope.' (There are six ancient and two modern alehouses in Roxeth, and there was a Roxeth roadsweeper who put his barrow in the blue ribboned army).

1503 Fishing in the pond on Roxeth common was forbidden. (This pond was replaced first by a Horses Trough and then by a busmen's clocking-in apparatus. It was at the bottom of West Street, adjoining Roxeth Farm.

1521 William Cox was presented for allowing a horse having "Le Mangy" to cross Roxeth Common. (The common is now reserved for white and grey flannelled cricketers).

1550 Henry Bette was presented for not stopping the water running from the pond called St. Edmunds Pond. (This pond which runs and overflows through our history was situated at Roxeth corner, and up to 1850, when it was in a very filthy condition, it was used for washing horses).

The Harrow Church Registers began in 1558. There are frequent references in them to the Blunts, the Greenehills, and other old established Roxeth families. Each section of the great archepiscopal Manor had its own local families. In addition to the Harwes of Harwe and the Roxethes of Roxeth there were the Flambards and Gerrards of Harrow, the Dudleys, the Pitts, the Greenehills and the Blunts of Roxeth, the Pages of Sudbury and the Catholic Bellamies of Uxendon.

But whilst the Bellamies, the Gerrards, and other families were losing their heads or their lands espousing lost causes, the Blunts and the Greenehills remained in quiet possession of their rich Roxeth land. A John Greenehill stood possessed of Roxeth soil when the Wars of the Roses broke out in the streets of St. Albans in 1455.

No doubt the battles at Barnet and the burnings at Smithfield were discussed at the Archery Butts and at Dobbs Mill, whilst the King's corn was being ground ; but these events did not stop an heir of the Blunts of Roxeth being baptised with due ceremonial in St. Mary's Church in 1565.

In 1586 William Greenehill of ROXEY was a Governor of Harrow School, and more than two centuries later these Greenehills and Blunts were still in firm possession of their Roxeth heritage. The names Mary Blunt, Henry Greenhill and Samuel Greenhill are written large across Dobbs Field, Newton Field and Hillfield in the Enclosure award map (M.R. 6) of 1818. (See back end paper.)

In 1850 three Greenhills still appear in the Roxeth directory. Mrs. Greenhill of Roxeth Villas is there, included with the Roxeth gentry, and Joseph Greenhill of Roxborough Farm is included amongst the Roxeth traders. Mrs. Chapman (nee Greenhill) was still the crinolined mistress of Roxeth Grange when the interesting engraving opposite page 63 was made. Dynasties disappeared and crops changed, but Roxeth's moated Grange remained ; and the Greenhill's held on to their Roxeth land.

CHAPTER FOUR

THE BREAK-UP OF THE MEDIAEVAL MANORS

(Cranmer to Wesley)

ON the 21st November, 1544, Thomas Cranmer, Archbishop of Canterbury, surrendered the avowson of the Harrow Rectory to Henry VIII. That was not sufficient, and on the 25th December, 1545, the majestic Lord who broke the bonds of Rome, again interfered to some effect in the affairs of the ancient manors of Hearge and Hroces-Seath, whose connections with Canterbury date back to the Ninth century. On that day Cranmer surrendered Canterbury's eight hundred year tenure of Harrow lands to Henry VIII. This transfer brought the mediæval part of the story of Herga and its satallite manors to an abrupt end.

Tradition says that this new Royal Lord of the manor visited his newly acquired property and that the royal hunting horns echoed round our hills and valleys. These stories, and one of a meeting with Wolsey who rode up from Headstone to meet his master on the hilltop, are supported by Henry's portrait on the village green and by the date writ large on the King's Head Hotel. Early in 1547 King Henry granted the Harrow manor to Sir Edward North and Lady North. This new Lord of the Manor next secured a main interest in the Harrow Rectory Manor, though certain tythes, including the important one of the Roxeth hay, were retained by the Dean and Chapter of Christ Church, Oxford.

With one brief lapse Sir Edward retained the favour of his fickle master and he appears as one of the executors of the will of Henry VIII. He gave his support to the plot to put Lady Jane Grey on the throne but he was forgiven by Queen Mary and made Lord North of Kirtling. When Elizabeth first came to London as Queen, entertainment and hospitality was provided for her by Lord North at the Charterhouse. Here, too, his son Thomas made the splendid translation of " Plutarchs Lives " which Shakespeare used in " Coriolanus " and other plays and which thus became everyman's most vivid introduction to the ancient world of noble Greeks and Romans. The Harrow manors were held almost in their entirety by the Norths and the Dudleys until 1630 ; but the Harrow Mediæval state was disintegrating, and poor laws and vagrant acts were powerless to hold it together. Some of the new Tudor Landed Gentry—the squires and yeomen who took over from the land owning barons and abbots, farmed their land well.

One, named John Lyon, from the produce of his farm at Preston was able to leave lands to a corporation "for a free grammar school for the poor, for poor scholars at universities and for repairing highways." One of his ancestors bearing the same honoured name—'John Lyon,' held land in Roxey as early as 1456, and the connection between Roxeth and the school was cemented by the choice of Thomas Page of Roxey as builder of Harrow School. He was paid £306 16s. 6d. straight away so that he could get on with the job.

They farmed and builded better than they knew. The Preston endowed Roxey built school has become famous. It has nourished six Prime Ministers and packed many Cabinets. In 1803 it was awarded the local children's, now much needed, common playing field (see back end paper) and it has since preserved the Hill by setting its own green belt of three cricket fields and thirty-four footer pitches round Harrow steeple.

With the possible exception of Pinner, none of the hamlets or manors around the hill had such rich soil or such extensive common lands as Roxey. Maps show that it remained largely unhedged, and that the mediæval practice of cultivation in long strips continued. When land was sold it was sold in "sellions"—the long strips between the furrows. Some land-owners were becoming interested in how the waste and common land near their property was being used. In 1629 Court Roll instructions were issued that erections on the lords' waste at Roxeth should be pulled down, and in 1681 a survey of waste lands at Roxeth and other places was made. Another survey was made of the lands of Grandfather Pitt of The Grange, who spent a good number of his four score years in litigation with the Gerrards of Flambards: the struggle between the hill and the vale was beginning. In 1630 the Dudleys sold their Roxeth Manor.

It is not surprising that the great landlocked rural Harrow area took a leading part in the fight against Ship Money and that destraints against yeomen of Pinner, Roxeth and Harrow for non-payment were many. In 1639 forty distresses on this account were taken out at Harrow alone. When Charles I finally broke with Parliament, gentry from Marylebone, Headstone and Northolt followed him to Oxford; but Roxeth seems to have gone against him and no doubt farm hands from St. Hildas, Eastcroft, The Grange, The Grove and other Roxeth localities enlisted in the Middlesex Regiment which Sir Gilbert Gerrard raised for Parliament.

On the 27th April, 1646, Charles I galloped up Northolt Road. The old route from Harrow to Uxbridge ran via Roxeth Green, Stroud Gate, Dobbs Mill Lane, Cut Lane and Golden Bridge and not via Woodend Lane or Ruislip. Tradition says that he rested awhile on the well at the top of Grove Hill. There is no tradition that Cromwell stabled his horses in Harrow Church ; but Charles II looking across the open fields from Windsor to Harrow saw St. Mary's on the hilltop. Its white spire, a pinnacle on a precipice, gleamed then, as now, in the sunlight and drove the merrie monarch to the conclusion that there was a " Church Visible " upon earth. There is no record that Queen Anne visited Roxeth, but tradition says that St. Hilda's and the Great Barn of Roxeth were built before she died.

The eighteenth century was the century of Walpole (let sleeping dogs lie), and Wesley (the world is my parish). At Harrow, as elsewhere, it was marked by a great falling off of the influence of the church and an increase in drinking and fox-hunting. The Inventory of the Church Goods at Harrow made in 1552 proves how rich and splendid the old ceremonial services in St. Mary's Harrow must have been. In the eighteenth century the ground floor of its tower was used to house the fire brigade, and when a church collection was taken up pewter plates for this purpose were borrowed from the nearest alehouse. Largely because the Roxeth hay and other great tithes were not paid, the church was unused and fell into a terrible state of disrepair. By 1786 every window in the church was broken.

And in those days came John Wesley to Roxeth to preach the Gospel in its great red tiled Manor Barn. He made the journey to and from the house of his friends at Eastcote by pleasant bridle paths across the Bonefield and Roxeth's broad hay-fields. For centuries this Great barn had been the rallying point of the Roxeth community. It is centrally near the junction of Roxeth's three tythings—" Newton," " Dobbs " and " Heath," and long before the erection of this barn or the others that preceeded it, or even before the ancient moat nearby was dug, it may have been the starting point for Roman festival processions ; the meeting place of the Saxon village moot, the place where our three mediaeval tything men forgathered after visiting the Manor Court, (or " Le Alehoope "). The present structure measuring one-hundred feet by sixty feet was certainly the gathering place for red-coated huntsmen, for ranters, preachers, tramps and hay-makers ; and less than a century ago it functioned as the Parish Hall for the whole neighbourhood. Here before Roxeth had a gasometer or South Harrow a tube station, Shakespeare was produced. Here, in my memory, Sunday School children collected for their Sunday School treats. Here, during the war of 1939—1945, came the Roxeth Boy Scouts dragging trek carts loaded with waste paper salvaged for the war effort. At different times it has been stacked with hay or golden grain to a height of sixty-six feet. It has frequently been described as the biggest barn in Middlesex and quite recently by a reputable evening paper as the biggest barn in England! It has a marvellous wide span of a roof, and the absence of supporting central pillars makes it possible for a coach

(*Engraved by* P. Lightfoot *from Painting of* 1504 *at Wroxham Abbey*)

Edward North

Thomas Cranmer

25th December, 1545
The Mediaeval Story Ends

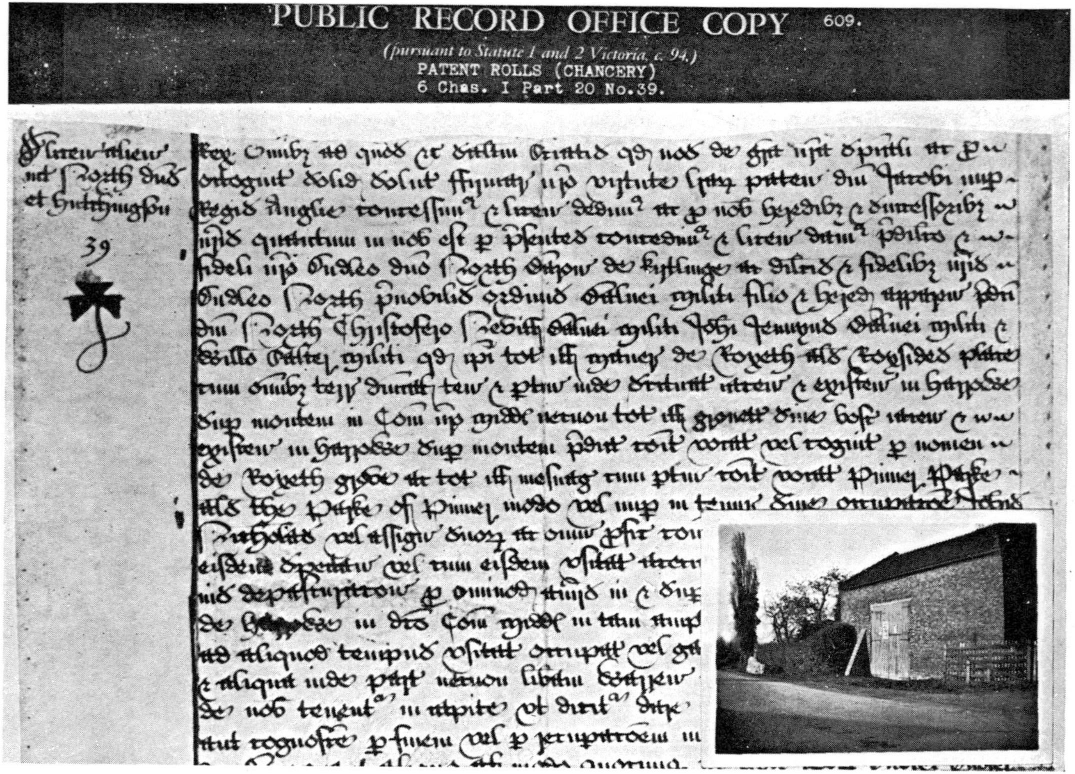

SALE OF ROXETH MANOR, 7-8 JANUARY, 1630
(Inset Tythe barn—a link with the Rectorial tythes and A.D. 845)

and six horses to drive into it, turn round, and drive out again without touching a wall or a single post. Some of its beautiful hand-made tiles were blown off when a bomb fell nearby, but it has suffered more from surburban neglect than from bombing. Inertia is worse than warfare.

In 1795, Daniel Lysons published his famous " Environs of London." Volume two of this monumental work deals with Middlesex, whose history he brings down to that date. Having checked a number of his statements with land records that are treasured at the Middlesex Guildhall, it is fitting that he should be allowed to give his record of the Roxeth he knew in his own words :

" Harrow is ten miles from Tyburn turnpike. It has 13,600 acres of land, equal arable and pasture. The principal hamlets, etc., in this parish are Pinner, Roxey or Roxeth, Wembley, Weald, Apperton, Kenton and Preston. Harrow is said in Warherdus' (Abbot Werhard) will to contain a hundred and four hides. These estates continued in the North family until the year 1630 when the avowson of the church and the rents of assize belonging to the manors of Woodhall, Hegeston and Roxeth were aliened by Dudley, Lord North to Edmund George Pitt and Rowland Pitt. They came afterwards to the Rushout family. The tenants' services due formerly in this manor seem to have been commuted for certain sums of money called ' work-silver ' which is frequently mentioned in the old survey.

ROXETH MANOR

The lands of Hamon and Hugh de Rokesie of this manor are mentioned in the endowment of Harrow Vicarage about 1240. In the year 1371 William Whittlesey, Archbishop of Canterbury, granted all the estates of William Roxethe, who had been outlawed for felony, to Sir Nicholas Brembre and his wife Idonea and their heirs. This estate seems to have reverted to the Archbishop for it appears to have been among the lands possessed by the North family and was aliened by Dudley, Lord North anno 1630 to John Hutchinson and others, being then called the Manor of Roxeth, alias Roxside Place. (Pat. 6, Car. pt. 20, No. 39).* In 1677 it was aliened by John Hutchinson to Robert Nichols Esq. Thomas Nichols died seised of it in 1705. It was conveyed in 1727 by the devisees under his will (after a suit in the Court of Chancery) to Thomas Brian, Esq. (This Thomas Brian was allowed to build himself a pew in Harrow Church on condition that he put out a poor parish boy to prentice). Brian Taylor, Esq., in the year 1764 aliened it to the late Percival Hart, Esq., (Record in the register of Deeds of Middlesex) whose widow now holds a third of it in dower. The remainder is the joint property of Emma, wife of David Garrick, Esq., (nephew of the celebrated David Garrick) and Mary, relict of Charles Vaughan Blunt . . . "

* Illustration opposite

To bring Lyson's story forward we may add the larger section became the property of R. B. Chapman by his marriage with the only daughter and heiress of William Greenhill.

Though the Chapmans were not such an ancient Roxeth family as the Blunts or the Greenhills, they wrote their name large across Roxeth's nineteenth century history. Different members of the family held farms and were responsible for the drainage of the whole area, while others controlled the Gas Works and interested themselves in local government and social welfare. Mr. John Chapman of the Gas Works presented Roxeth with its first Mission Hall and the Harrow Urban District Council with its first Chairman's Chain of Office.

Roxeth Manor, like Roxeth itself, appears under several names ; most commonly the alternative or bracket name with the Manor is Roxeth Place. Sometimes it is called Roxside Place or Roxades.

Except for Wesley's preaching and the burning of a Harrow School governor's coach on Roxeth Common, the story of this hay-making hamlet in the eighteenth century seems to have been singularly uneventful. Roxeth became one of those happy places which had no recorded history. Occasionally there was an exodus of young men from its fields and farms, and the 'old uns' were hard put to it to get in all the hay. If you had asked in those days where George was, you would have found that like his predecessor the Saint he had gone to fight another dragon. Sometimes it was a French one, sometimes a Russian, sometimes a German. George felt that his country and his village were something worth fighting for. So he sang "Boney was a warrior!" and went off to the wars longing for the day when he could get back to the barns and the hayricks of good old Roxey!

CHAPTER FIVE

THE DISMEMBERMENT OF ROXETH

(*George III to Victoria*)

WE now come to one of the least satisfactory chapters in the story of Roxeth. In the nineteenth century Roxeth was dismembered. In the twentieth century its ancient good name was almost taken away.

In the year 1800 George III mounted on horseback in a Windsor uniform with a pig-tail, refreshed himself at the sign of the King's Head on the village green, whilst a holiday was arranged for the School. At that time the view from the King's Head to the village pump house at the top of West Street was interrupted only by a wheelwright's shed in which the boys got their hoops mended. A post-chaise was kept at the King's Head and three times a week a coach from Harrow ran through fields to London the nearest place where a hot bath could be obtained.

The route from Harrow turnpike to the goldfinch fields near Paddington is delightfully described in a rather pious tract dated 1805, which also illustrates how great was the gulf between the illiterate poor and the educated gentry, when the Cunninghams preached at St. Mary's and the Druries mastered the Hill.

The church was regaining its good name and the school was growing in strength ; but wealth and strength are not everything : the battle of the classes, the rich and the poor, the enfranchised and the unenfranchised was beginning. Tenant's service had been commuted for ' work-silver,' but the labourer on the land was still having a thin time and Parliament was still made up almost entirely of landowners.

ENCLOSURES

It is said that the greatest changes in the character and appearance of the English countryside between the Dissolution of the Monasteries and the opening of the Great Exhibition are tied up with the word " enclosure."

Roques Map of Middlesex (1745) and a map of the Harrow Desmesne lands dated 1759 by Issac Messner, show the shape and the enormous size of the three unhedged Roxeth common fields ; the width of the village green ; and how most of the roads were bordered by wide strips of waste land. Roxeth still extended from Stroud Gate to Roxborough Gate and there were common field

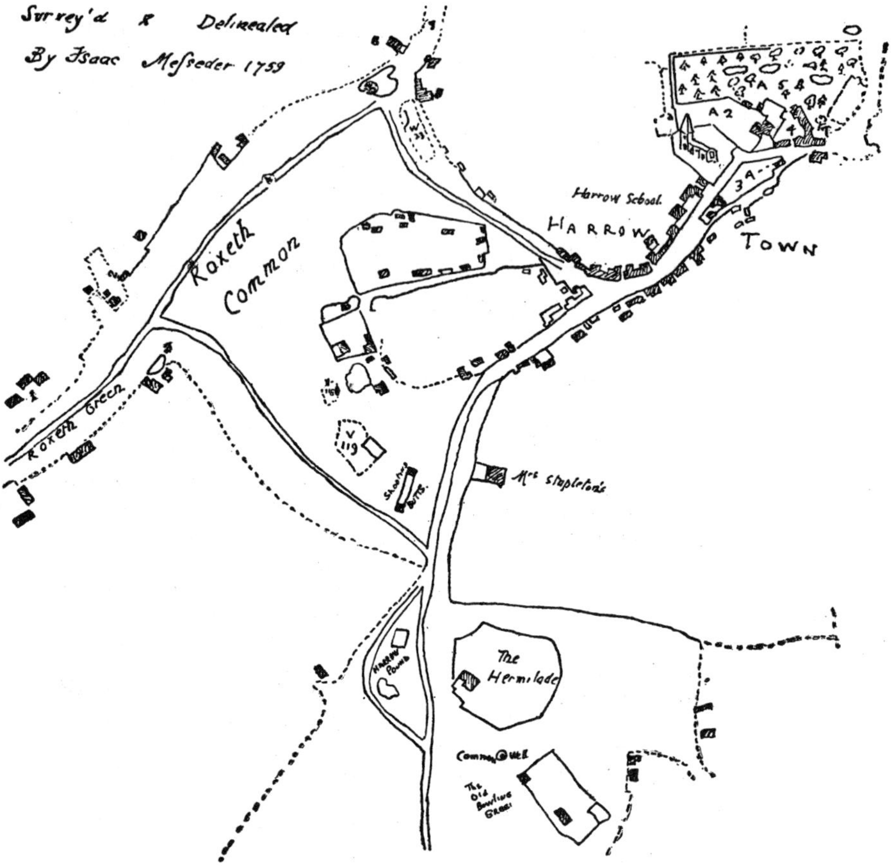

(1) Roxeth Moat, Barn and Grange (2) Dudley Lodge (3) Half Moon Shaped Pond (4) and (7) Roxeth Road (5) The Horse Pond (6) Roxeth Farm (8) Roxeth House.

areas both to the north and the south of the hamlet. The extensive area bounded by Roxeth Hill, Crown Street and Lower Road was shewn as Roxeth Common and " Les Buttez in Roxeth " (the shooting butts) were still shewn at the top of Roxeth Hill.

A coloured map of the Harrow enclosure Award (58 George IIII 1818, Hilary Rot. 78) may be seen at the Public Records Office. On this the Common Fields are shewn in red and the Common Land in green. A few blue coloured areas (there is one at The Grange) indicated old enclosures which were subject to Corn Rent and a few yellow coloured areas (there is one at Dudley Lodge) shew old enclosures that had been exchanged.

The great red coloured area of Roxeth's COMMON FIELDS stretches from The Grange to the Eastcote and Northolt boundaries.

The three main divisions are labelled Hill Field, Newton Field, and Dabbs Field. Hill Field adjoins The Grange, and the biggest allotment of them went to Henry Greenhill. In Newton Field 368 acres are marked Rectorial tythes. An arm of this field (where Tythe Farm stands) penetrates into and links up the other Common Fields. Allotments to two old Roxeth families, the Blunts and the Greenhills, are dispersed in a most interesting manner in each of the main divisions of the Great Roxeth Common field area. (See end cover).

THE COMMON LAND is coloured green ; and broad and narrow strips which stretch from Roxeth Corner to Stroud Gate along both sides of the now dangerously narrow Northolt Road are labelled Roxeth Green. These strips were awarded to R. Wilson, F. Hollis, I. Jones and other Roxeth farmers and landowners. In contrast to these strips a great solid block of green COMMON stretched from the Butts at the top of Roxeth Hill to Roxeth House at the bottom of West Street. The top part of this Common land round the crest of Roxeth Hill was awarded to Lord Northwick, Lord of the Harrow Manor. The central and lower part went to the Governors of Harrow School. The large piece (415) labelled Playground was enclosed and became the famous Harrow School Cricket Ground.

The property owning governors had the authority of a property owning House of Commons for enclosing this ground, but for half a century the Roxeth Common enclosure was stoutly resisted by the locals. Fights between Harrovian cricketers and Roxeth chaws were frequent. In one of these Byron, who was a ringleader in all school games and mischief, came into serious conflict with an angry young farmer and it is said that he owed his life to the timely intervention of his friend Cecil Tattersall who warded off the blow. By the time Queen Victoria came to the throne a better feeling between the school and the more respectable townsfolk was developing, and Dr. Vaughan did what he could to foster this.

Many interesting sidelights on the countryside round Harrow come from the Schoolboy diary of Walter Trevelyan. Like Sir William Jones (the oriental scholar who was a boy at Harrow in 1752) he made the fields round the Hill his own, but in a rather different way. Instead of giving certain Roxeth fields the names of Greek states and claiming a boyish military and political suzeranity over them, he studied their natural beauty and the passage of the seasons through them. Walter Trevelyan kept his diary from 1812—1815, the years when the Middlesex Regiment were winning their " Die Hard " name in the Peninsula War. He records not only the battles in the Peninsula and the rows with the locals in the cricket fields, but the peace that abided in the footpath fields beyond them. The red squirrels and the woodpeckers he watched in the churchyard, " 26th June, 1815, whole holiday for victories. The birds began to sing at half past two in the morning." He found Oxlips at Dabbs Hill on 2nd May and I can testify that they were to be found in the same field a century later.

SCHOOLS

Just as some folk were becoming reconciled to the enclosure of Roxeth Common another dispute between the School Governors and the local residents was brought to a head by the 1810 Inquiry into the original nature of the John Lyon Foundation and the present mode of conducting the school.

" This celebrated seminary—one of the eight principal public schools in the Kingdom—has not escaped the usual fate of eminent success in producing murmurs from the envious or the ill-informed. Certain inhabitants of Harrow had long felt a strange displeasure at its growing fame and wished to confine its advantages within their ancient narrow bounds " . . . So wrote J. Norris Brewer in 1816 and it is interesting to note that in that year only three local boys attended the " free grammer schoole " which John Lyon had endowed primarily for the good of the parish. The remaining 295 were non-parishioners.

These rich " foreigners " (John Lyon's word for non-parishioners) called the few remaining local boys " charity home bugs," but they made good use of the local common and the local endowment. Except for Parr's rebellion, and the burning of the Governors Coach, Wellington's Waterloo training might have been completed on the Roxey playing fields. Then as top school boys became generals, cardinals, authors, colonial governors and Prime Ministers, they carried the fame of Harrow to the ends of the earth. The School Governors were consolidated in their hold of the Hill, the Common, and the Endowment by the Enclosure Act of 1803, by the judgment of Sir William Grant, Master of the Rolls in 1810 and by the Public School Act of 1865.

When the controversy to confine John Lyon's Charity within its ancient parochial limits was at its height, " a parochial school for gratuitious instruction " was set up on Roxeth Hill. It was founded largely through the exertions of the Rev. J. W. Cunningham (Vicar of Harrow 1811—1861) and was organised on the sectarian lines recommended by the Rev. Doctor Andrew Bell who wrote in his " An Experiment in Education "—' It is not proposed that the children of the poor be educated in an expensive manner or even taught to write or to cypher. Parents will always be found to educate at their own expense enow to fill the stations which require higher qualifications (Dr. Bell successfully held eight army chaplaincies at the same time) and there is a risk of elevating by indiscrimate education the minds of those doomed to the drudgery of daily labour above their condition and thereby rendering them discontented or unhappy in their lot."

The expenses of the church or national school on Roxeth Hill were defrayed by subscription, and about 170 children took benefit of it. Subsequently this establishment was taken over by " The Board " and it now functions as Roxeth Hill Council School. One of its first inspectors was Matthew Arnold, the poet, who then lived two fields away from this School at Byron House. He was one of the earliest champions of "secondary" education and he emphasised "that system, concert and thought were required to provide every part of the country with the highly differentiated organisation necessary to ensure to every child the particular kind of schooling it needs."

Roxeth Hill School contains a plaque and a room dedicated to the memory of Lord Shaftesbury's son. The inscription reads: "This school room is built in memory of the Honourable Antony Francis Henry Ashley who died at Harrow in the faith of Lord Jesus Christ, May 31st, 1849, aged 16 years and two months. Those that seek Me early will find Me." Lord Shaftesbury's long sustained fight for the oppressed began when he was a boy at Harrow, as he witnessed the passing of a pauper's funeral. A plaque in the ancient red bricks of Harrow School "Love-Serve" commemorates this event and a road cut through the heart of old Roxeth bears Shaftesbury's name.

Dr. C. J. Vaughan, who was Harrow's greatest master, as Shaftesbury was one of its greatest pupils, attempted to reconcile the legal claims of the Governors with the moral claims of the residents for a share in the John Lyon bequest by establishing "The English Form." Although he and other ordained Headmasters meant well, their proposals were not well received and were called "shams, baits, bribes." Nevertheless the Lower School of John Lyon which stands on the edge of the ecclesiastical boundary between Harrow and Roxeth served a useful purpose for many years; and when it contained all the Perrins of Sudbury, the six sons of Farmer Priest of Roxey and all the Parkhouses of Pinner, it must have been a school near to the heart of Yeoman John Lyon of Preston. Until recently, and thanks largely to the generosity of Mr. T. F. Blackwell of Stanmore, the Lower School found room amongst its fee payers for a few scholarship boys from Roxeth Hill and other schools of more modern growth. This was fortunate, for the gap—between the proud school which gave a select few all that money could buy, and the federation of state schools which aimed at giving increased opportunities to Everyman—was widening. During the last hundred years only one boy has passed from Roxeth Hill School, via the Lower School to the top school, the varsity and an assistant commissionership in India. He was certainly not the only local boy capable of profiting by a classical education or by the Fourth Form training of a John Smith. In the meantime Roxeth, good old Roxey, which provided the top church with so much of its endowment and the top school with its world famous cricket ground, has no grammar school and is very inadequately provided with open spaces for its growing children.

At the census of 1831 ROXETH HAMLET had a population of 842 in 153 houses, and Harrow hamlet a population of 1359 in 167 houses. More than half this population was still employed in agriculture.

A hundred years ago, on 10th November, 1848, from the large

tombstone under which John Peachy was ' buried in the woollen ' and on which Byron often reclined, Queen Victoria looked down on Roxeth before continuing her journey to the Dowager Queen Adelaide at Bentley Priory. At that time the Peachy stone had no iron cage and Roxeth no gasometer. It was an unspoiled, independant and very beautiful hamlet ; and as the following list of its gentry and tradespeople shows, it was still possible to know the names and the occupations of everyone who lived in the village.

The nine GENTRY were John Duncan Esq., Rev. and Mrs. Isaac S. Gale, *Dudley Cottage* Curate, Mrs. Greenhill *Roxeth Villa*, Mrs. Heathfield *Raleigh Cottage*, E. Humphreys Esq., *Roxeth Cottage* Mrs. Pigou *Roxeth Villas*, George Webster Esq. *Roxeth Villas*, Captain George C. Wynne *Roxeth House* (later called *The Capers*).

The twenty-eight TRADERS were Charles Atkins, Farmer ; George Atkins, Timber and Coal Merchant, *Roxborough* ; John Atkins, Beer Shop Keeper, " *Timber Truck* "; Jas. Ball " *Three Horse Shoes* "; Joseph Baker, Farmer ; William Baker, Farmer ; Mrs. Butterfield, Laundress ; Richard Chad, *Roxborough* Cricket Ground Keeper ; Richard Brown Chapman, Farmer, *The Grange* ; John Clayton, Farmer ; Thomas Cornwall, Beer Shop Keeper ; Abraham Farmborough, Beer Shop Keeper, " *Half Moon* "; Joseph Farmborough, Carpenter ; Charles Ceasar Greaves, Relieving officer ; Joseph Greenhill, Farmer, *Roxborough* ; John Hodson, Farmer ; Mrs. Howe, Laundress ; Jonathan Lambird, Butcher ; William Martin, Bricklayer ; William Martin, Pig Killer ; William Nobes, Farrier ; Mrs. Page, Laundress ; James Paine, Baker and Grocer ; James Parker, Farmer ; George Richins, Land Measurer and Collector of Poor Rates ; Mrs. Shepherd, Laundress ; Henry Way, Farmer and assessor of Land who assessed Taxes for Roxeth.

The proportionate respectability and importance of the hamlets surrounding the Hill at this time is indicated by the total numbers of gentry and trades included in the Directory.

	Gentry	Tradesmen
Roxeth	9	28
Greenhill	6	7
Wembley	4	13
Alperton		10
Kenton	1	4
Preston	1	4

The Harrow Handbook in which Thomas Smith incorporates these directories was published in 1850, and it includes much useful information on Roxeth : Miss Mary Ann Bryant, a famous story teller, was then mistress of Roxeth Infants School. Wesleys preaching in the Great Barn had not been in vain. Roxeth Church was unbuilt but the now derelict Wesleyan Church in Lower Road opposite the now devastated site of the old Roxeth Cottage Hospital was functioning. Rick fires were of frequent occurence, and the keys of the Fire Station in Hogarth Lane (Crown Street) could be obtained at the Police Station or if Mr. Hunsdon the village constable was out, at the " Crown " opposite. Mr. Chad was Keeper of the Cricket (Common) Field. Harrow Station was re-classified as First Class. A bus left Harrow at nine o-clock each morning for " The Bull " Holborn. " Another agreeable way of reaching London was by walking to Ealing and then taking the train to Paddington." A still more leisurely way was to walk to the " Black Horse " Greenford and wait for a Canal Boat. There were three official carriers Dixon, Hudson, and Kidney ; but a lot of goods found their way unofficially to London on the Roxeth Haycarts. In bad weather the drivers of these often took a whole day to make the return journey and they usually carried a great bundle of faggots to help them bridge holes in the roads, or get out of ancient ruts that the way wardens had left unfilled. The hamlets were entirely without public lighting, but they were watched by the Metropolitan Police Force at a cost of £1,025 from the poor Rates. The Highway rate was fourpence in the pound, and all highways except the turnpikes were in the care of elected non-professional surveyors. Amongst the local trades practised were Hayseller, Straw hat maker, Bird Stuffer, Dairy woman, Chandler, Cheesemonger, Hurdle Maker, Dealer in Faggots, Land Measurer and Pig Killer. Thomas Ship Grimwade is stated in prominent italics to be the Inventor of Condensed Milk and Antony H. Gibson was the Bath Keeper. " Baths and Douches on the Hydropathic principle were now available." Harrow was looking up, but there was still a serious shortage of water. The town pump working sixteen strokes a minute delivered 150 gallons an hour (when it was working). William Martin, the Roxeth Pig Killer, and sundry other residents had private wells, and the houses of the rich had the usual provision for the storage of rain water. I still have the silicated carbon filter through which my parents strained the water they obtained from the pond across the road.

ADMINISTRATION CHANGES

It was this water shortage which led to the assimilation of Roxeth into Harrow and to its use as a dump and sewer farm for the overcrowded town where the young gentlemen resided. Up to 1850 government of Harrow hamlet and Roxeth hamlet was of the village type and was largely regulated by overseers of the poor, surveyors of highways and those very ancient local government officials—the church wardens.

Harrow had long been reckoned a healthy locality, but the school medical officer of 1849 and other propertied residents were concerned about its water supply, its drainage and its sanitation. An Enquiry was accordingly held in 1849 at the King's Head, and evidence showed that near the houses of the Harrow Headmaster and the Roxeth pig killer, conditions were hardly sanitary.

The report made on this Enquiry by G. T. Clarke, the superintending inspector, is extremely interesting ; for it gives information about the topography, geology, history, population and government of the district before it proceeds to the map and the recommendations that a new and defined area should come under the Public Health Act provisions and be administered by nine gentlemen, each possessed of the maximum property qualification.

The new area was given the new name Harrow-on-the-Hill, although the incorporated slice of Roxeth was bigger then Harrow itself. Remaining chunks of Roxeth, already separated by the enclosure of 1803, came under the Hendon Rural District. There is a lot which is best left unsaid about the Herga-Hroces Seath combination by which Roxeth got the corporation dust, the snow-sweepings from the hill, the sewage, the gasworks, the laundry, the isolation hospital, and the pre-fabs, whilst younger sections of the new Harrow urbanity got the top and the secondary schools, the libraries and the sunlight and fresh air which comes from wide open spaces.

It would be wrong to suggest that Roxeth got nothing out of the deal. It had tap water, street lamps and a horse bus to connect it with a railway station nearby fifty years before Northolt ; and the conditions set out in the following extract from the 1849 Report were improved when Roxeth was incorporated and partly urbanised :

> " From the old toll bar a steep road, London Hill, descends towards Roxeth. On its north side above the National Schools is a filthy pond, the overflow of which is led down the roadside by a ditch now partially covered in. Opposite is a row of cottages with an open somewhat filthy ditch behind. The people there are chiefly supplied with water from a well ten and a half feet deep in William Martins' garden. The rent here is about 2/6d a week. At the angle of Roxeth Road with London Hill is a small and very filthy pond used for washing horses but in summer too filthy even for this. Upon this same road on the outskirts of the town near the Three Horse Shoes is a farmhouse with a very large dung heap between the front window and the public way. The whole tract is low, damp and undrained. Ascending from the horse pond towards the town pump the road much needs repair."

Since 1859 Harrow has been continuously and well served by its own weekly newspaper. In one of the earliest issues correspondents suggested that the abundance of green lanes at Roxeth was responsible for an excess of gypsies and beggars on the Hill and that Roxeth should be provided with a parish church.

By 1860 a gas lighted Public Hall opposite the " Kings Head " was competing with Roxey's Great Barn as a place of entertainment.

In 1863 the great ecclesiastical parish of Roxeth was formed. The new parish church on Roxeth Hill opposite the National Schools gave an increased sense of unity to the scattered hamlet, and before the end of the century Roxeth had the finest and the largest Parish Hall in the district.

In 1888 the Middlesex County Council assumed responsibility for many of the Roxeth's local services which had been discharged in days gone by through tything men, beadles, wardens, and parish officials. In 1894 the Harrow Urban District Council was formed. It took over the administration of old Harrow hamlet plus Roxeth and Greenhill Green. Then in 1934 when Pinner, Wealdstone and other hamlets were added to Harrow and Roxeth, the new administrative area began to have some resemblance in size to the old Archbishops Manor as scheduled in the Doomsday record and some resemblance in shape to the Northern Pagus of the old Roman territorium of London.

TRANSPORT CHANGES

But greater changes than those due to, or controllable by, administration were taking place. As the decades of the 19th Century swept by, new methods of transport brought Roxeth closer to the Metropolis and increased the number and importance of its contacts with the outside world. Trains competed with stage coaches. Then as motors followed steam trains Uncle Ned stopped taking articles for repair to London on his hay cart. Finally air liners, carrying distinguished visitors, roared out of the sky above a Roman like viaduct which carried electric tube trains across the submerged site of the old stockaded village in the rook marshes.

On 22nd July, 1801, Lord Palmerston, who was then a boy at Harrow School, witnessed the taking of the first tolls at the Harrow Turnpike. This was set close to the old Archery Butts at the top of Roxeth Hill and Betsey Wootton mounted guard over it until at the advanced age of 105 she was laid to rest in Roxeth Churchyard. The days when the Lord of the Manor could obtain the materials, the carts and the labour for repairing the roads were past, and the coming of the Turnpike roads took a big burden off the waywardens. Harrow School Governors and boys seem to have resisted the march of time towards their hill sanctuary. In 1812 the boys mobbed a party of 60 dissenters who had come by canal boat from Paddington to Greenford Green (return fare 2/6) to be present at the opening of the new Baptist Chapel in Byron Hill, and a few years later the white fence opposite the Headmasters house was spotted with the blood of four navvies of the London and Birmingham Railway who came into conflict with the Harrow boys. This episode did not stop the Harrow and Wealdstone Station being opened in 1837. The train service from Harrow on the Hill to Baker Street dates from 1880 but the trams got no farther than Sudbury at the foot of Harrow Hill.

A Jubilee was followed by a Diamond Jubilee but Roxeth remained rural and continued to supply its quota of milk and good Middlesex hay until horses were replaced in the London Streets by Motor Cars (" those smelly sparrow starvers!"). Grove Hill was the scene of the first fatal motor accident in this country.

On 23rd June, 1903 the first electric train ran from a station labelled "South Harrow for Roxeth and Northolt" through Sudbury *Hill* Station (built across a *valley* and formerly known as Greenford Road) to Mill Hill Park Station now called Acton Town. Perhaps the most absurd bit of new railway place naming was North Harrow (..Headstone) which lies almost due West of West Harrow Station. Hot water, electric light in the hall, Harrow headed note paper, and other surburban amenities followed quickly in the path of the electric railway, and Roxeth was cut into 'desirable' South Harrow building plots.

Three great powers, the London Transport Board, Holy Church and the Harrow Urban District Council seemed set on making an end of Roxeth, and quite unwittingly they combined to take away first its good name, then its unity and lastly its sunlight. Yet I have a presentiment that the story of Roxeth is not ended.

The Phoenix of the ash heap is stretching her wings. She has celebrated her XI Centenary ; and having persuaded the greatest urban authority in the kingdom to replace two of her ancient boundary marks, and having stated her case at the Ward Boundary Enquiry, in 1948, she may yet go forward as the oldest partner in Lanfranc's Manor and achieve for her three wards something like Borough Status alongside Pinner, Weald, and Stanmore in the Harrow *County* Borough which is yet to be.

In Persia there is a mythological bird. In Egypt a mythological God. One had a faculty of reappearing after it had been cremated. The other a habit of coming to life after it had been dismembered by the very highest authorities. Oh Phoenix! Oh Osiris! So let it be with Roxeth.

ROXETH HISTORY IN HERALDRY

From the surveying tripod of Frontinus the eye glimpses eight boundary marks enclosing the Newton, Dobbs, and Heath tythings. Like the ravens of Odin, the Roxeth rooks look back and remember. The Mercian saltire of Offa offsets the Wessex dragon of Werembert, whose Roxeth lands pass in A.D .845 to Wergard of Christ Church.

The paths of goodness and greatness mount upward. The sword divides. The cross unites. The pallium of the Archbishop supports the cross of Christ Church. The three choughs of Becket are overwhelmed by the three Royal lions. Roxeth divided by Frontinus and linked by Christ Church brings the tythed shuck of Newton and the milled corn of Dobbs to build up and be built up by St. Mary's. Brembre's manor passes to the Norths and the Dudleys. Rooted in charity the School expands. Robbed of its Common and incorporated in Harrow's health system, Christ Church parish survives and shines with Pinner, Harrow, Wealdstone, and Stanmore as one of the five stars in the ancient visible celestial crown of St. Mary's. "And I will make them and the places round my hill a blessing." (*Ezekiel* 36.)

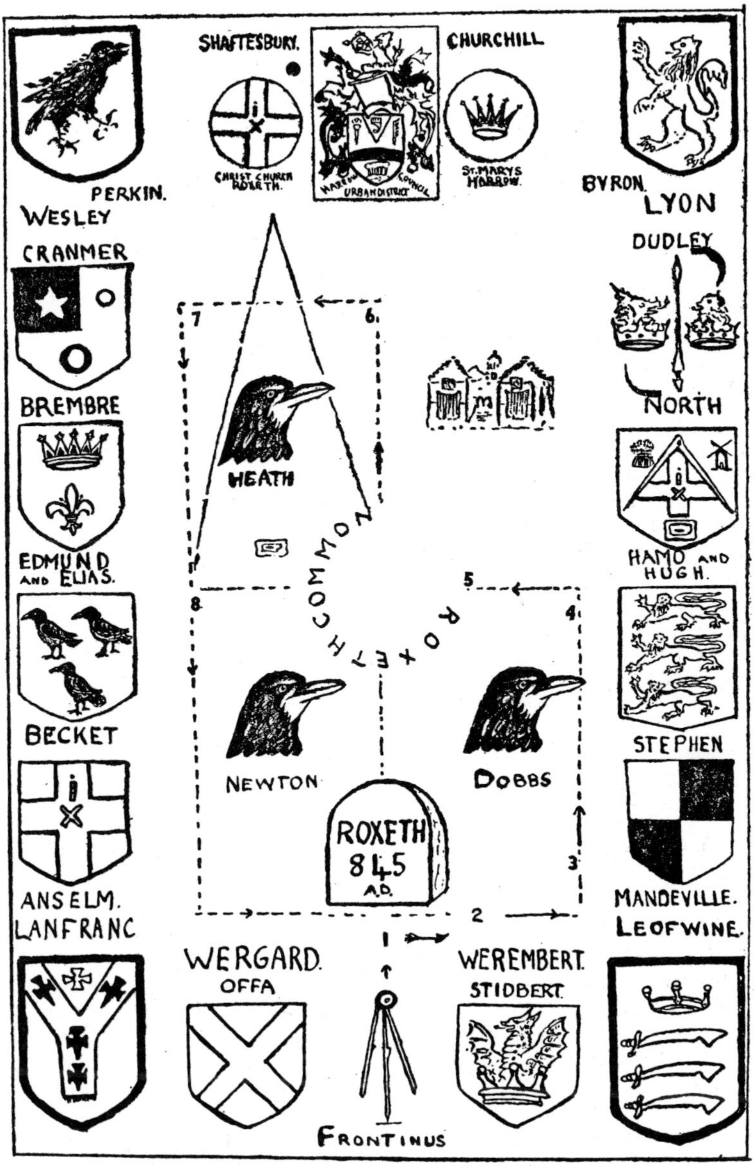

ROXETH HISTORY IN HERALDRY.

PART II. THE SPIRIT OF ROXETH

" Will no one tell me what she sings ?
Perhaps the plaintive numbers flow
For old, unhappy, far of things
And battles long ago."

CHAPTER SIX

THE THANE OF ROXEY

(A.D. 845)

Written for the Hroces Seath XIth Centenary Celebrations and produced by Michael Stayre on 8th, 9th and 10th November, 1945, at St. Pauls Hall.

CASTE

WEREMBERHT, *Thane of Roxey*	W. E. WILLIAMSON
FREDA, HILDA, EDGAR, ATHELSTAN, *His grandchildren*	F. BARTLETT, R. WILDING, D. J. BARTLETT, J. BURNS
CEOLNOTH, *Archbishop of Canterbury* ..	E. HALL
CEOLBERT, *Bishop of London*	H. ROCK
WILRED, *Bishop of Dunwich*	E. SCHUTE
ALCHUN, *Bishop of Worcester*	T. BARTON
GUTHEARD, *Bishop of Selsey*	C. FORD
TATNOTH, *Bishop of Rochester*	J. A. LEIGH
BERETRED, *Bishop of Linsey*	F. KINGSTON
TUNBERT, *Bishop of Lichfield*	L. MITCHELL
HUNBERT, *Bishop of Elmham*	P. PIERCE
ABBOT WERHARD, *of Christ Church*	A. COOPER

PLACE

SCENE I is set in the fields that adjoin Roxeth's old Moat and ancestral barn.

SCENE II is set at Allhallows Berkinge Church, London, because St. Pauls had been wasted by fire in A.D. 842 and because its ancient Saxon doorway was brought to light by incendiary bombs on 30th December, 1940.

PLOT

Saxon children are playing in the fields we seek to preserve for the children of surburbia. Then, (as now) sinister influences are at work. Saxon openness is pitted against Latinised legality but the old name survives. The church gets and consecrates the land but the barn is preserved for the use of the parish.

TIME

The HROCES-SEATH parchement of 8th November, 845, is preserved at the British Museum. It is printed as No. 448 in Birch " Cartularium Saxonicum." The ancient episcopal see of Dunwich has been submerged by the encroaching tide, but Bishop Wilred's name survives on this trustworthy and authentic document, which lights up the very darkest days of the struggle between the English and the Danes. The voluble Anglo-Saxon Chronicle shrivels, and the story of the years 839 to 850 is told in eighty-four words.

839	This year there was great slaughter at London, Rochester and Canterbury.
840	This year King Ethewulf fought at Charmouth against the crews of 35 ships and the Danish men maintained possession of the field. And Louis the Emperor died.
841—844	No entry.
845	This year Eanwulf the earldorman with the men of Somerset and Bishop Ealstan, and Osric the earldorman with the men of Dorset fought at the mouth of the Parret against the Danish army and there made great slaughter and got the victory.
846—850	No entry.

So we turn to the HROCES-SEATH document for evidence that the Saxons were still in possession of London ; that Wessex and Mercian bishops both accept the Primacy of Canterbury ; that though bishoprics are being spoiled by the Danes the church militant is still acquiring land.

SCENE I. A Roxeth meadow in A.D. 845

Freda, a Saxon girl, is nursing a baby. Her cousin, Hilda is weaving a basket.

Enter Edgar and Athelston, two Saxon boys.

They are dragging a large toy whale boat.

Freda: Why are you dragging that about? You know that father won't let you have it here.

Edgar: Well, it can't stop in the barn. Brother Paulinus says we must not play in the barn.

Freda: And why mustn't we? It is our barn isn't it?

Ath: It was. But it has been taken over by the Church.

Edgar: By *Holy* Church Athelston! Let us forget about Paulinus. He is not the Church, and there are not many Brothers like him.

Ath: The dockéd cloisterer!

Edgar: Well, he does not own the sunlight ; and he can't stop us floyting and playing at Quarterstaff in the buttercup fields. Come on, I challenge you. (He throws down his staff. Athelston throws his across it. The girls pick them up and hand them to their champions and the duel begins).

Freda: Go it Edgar. Duck, quick, quicker.
Hilda: You can save your breath Freda, Athelston will win.
Freda: No he won't.
Hilda: Chance work is the best work.
Freda: Only when it happens right. Weight counts.
Hilda: Wait and see. (Edgar wins).
Freda: Wolf! I told you so.
Hilda: Don't crow too soon. That's only the first round. Anyway you can't do this. (Turns a cartwheel).
Freda: Don't show off Hilda.
Hilda: I shall, Athelston likes it, don't you Athelston?
Ath. Yes, but I don't like to see you cousins quarrelling.
Edgar: Nor do I.
Freda: Well, she started it.
Hilda: No I did not!
Edgar: Drop it, here comes one of the Brothers.
Ath: Not Paulinus, I hope. I could . . . (indicates his staff).
Edgar: Stop it, anger gets you nowhere. When you feel like that bite your tongue and sing.
(Voice off stage). Easie, easie, catchee mousie.
Ath: I believe it's . . .
Freda: Why, it's Uncle Eddy.
Edgar: So it is.
Hilda: So it is. Hurrah! (Turns somersault).
(Boys shake hands. Enter Brother Ceolbert).
Edgar: Can we have another whale hunt?
Hilda: No, lets climb trees and dance.
Ceolbert: I think it must be a whale hunt. You children overwhelm me like waves of the sea. I was travelling the seas last week.
Freda: (delighted). Have you been across the water to see the savage heathen again?
Ceolbert: Yes. I gave one of them your bracelet and she sent you this.
Freda: What is it?
Ceolbert: A sugar cane. On the way back I saw a great friend of yours.
Freda: Not Wilred? (Ceolbert nods).
Ceolbert: Yes, Wilred.
Edgar: Hurry up Athelston or we shall miss the whale. He's spouting again.
Ceolbert: Who me?
Edgar: No, the whale! (To Ath). You get ready the boat and call up the Roxey Boatmen. I will fetch the ropes, the harpoon and the tackle from the Barn.
Ath: Whooeee (Two more boys appear).
Edgar: (sings) Row Thorsmen, row.
All: Freya watches you

(*Photo by* F. WHITE)

THE GREAT BARN OF ROXETH, 100 FEET LONG, 60 FEET WIDE, 63 FEET HIGH, 1947

"It hurts me to give up the old barn, my father rebuilt it after Ellandune"

"REMEMBER THE BOY"
THE CHARLES GARDNER TOC H LAMP AT 6 CROWN STREET

THE 12TH HARROW (ROXETH CHURCH) SCOUTS
Need a field for their activities

Edgar: The storm clouds are rising
All: The Whales are in view
Edgar: The storm clouds are rising
All: The whales are in view . . .
Ceolbert: What divine imagination. Whale hunting on dry land! The sea is in their blood.
(Two lines of song repeated. Enter WEREMBERHT, King's Thane of Roxey).
Thane: Good morrow Brother Ceolbert.
Ceolbert: God bless you Thane Weremberht. I expect you are proud of these noisy grandchildren.
Thane: Yes, they are proper Roxey Boys. I have taught them to track and cook and rough it.
Ceolbert: I am glad to hear it. In these times the world needs strong men. Soon they will be sitting in your saddle and fighting as you have fought to preserve the things that make life worth living.
Edgar: Brother Paulinus says we must not fight at all.
Thane: It would be a thin world for Brother Paulinus if no-one did his share of the fighting.
Edgar: But I thought . . .
Thane: Don't interrupt.
Edgar: I wanted to get the right and the wrong of this fighting business.
Thane: You never will. When duty stares you in the face you must think fast and do the next thing, and it won't always be easy and pleasant.
(EDGAR Retires).
Thane: (To Ceolbert). I had the same perplexities myself when I was a boy. The soft music of the afterworld was loud in my ears. The incence was in my nostrils, but I came to my senses when this hamlet was burned to the ground. I have been talking to Wilred again. Now that he is Lord Bishop of Dunwich he wants me to appoint another parish priest for Roxey, but as he has been my chaplain and the parish priest so long I cannot think of it.
Ceolbert: That's a pity.
Thane: Are not twenty singing Brothers enough?
Ceolbert: No they are not. I know there can be no real successor to Wilred. He is part and parcel of Roxeth, but this ancient parish needs its own priest. Its a proud old place and it takes a lot of understanding.
Thane: That is why the Danes have always punished it so unmercifully, Wilred remembers the first burning after the Haest on the Hill even though he was only a child at the time. I am getting old myself and I want to do the right thing by this old place. I have at last agreed to Wilred's suggestion that the Brothers should have the

land near their settlement as booke-land. In exchange I shall take the fields at Greenford. Already they are green again after the battle.

Ceolbert: The good long suffering earth is very forgiving. It was a mighty deliverance you brought the trembling Brothers and the frightened children that day, Thane Werembert.

Thane: It was my stiffest fight.

Ceolbert: Your greatest hour.

Thane: I can still see them swarming out of their boats at Bregentaford. Every man had a new black rook helmet. We looked a rabble but we played cat and mouse with them, retreating slowly until they were well away from their boats. Then our hidden horsemen rode in, cut them off, and we dealt with them piecemeal in the marshes. Those helmets made a pretty pile at the end of the day. They were my share of the booty. I still have them. They may be needed one day.

Ceolbert: I hope not.

Thane: Edgar.

Edgar: Yes, Sire?

Thane: Fetch me one of those Danish rook helmets.
(Exit EDGAR).

Ceolbert: Will you make a new house at Greenford?

Thane: No! Greenford has too many houses already. Give me the wide open spaces—the woods—and the big Barns of old Roxey. I don't mind parting with the land, but it hurts me to give up the old Barn. My father rebuilt it after Ellandune.

Ceolbert: That was some time ago.

Thane: Yes, but I can't help thinking of those old unhappy days, when men knew right from wrong without parchments. Ella's word was his bond.

Ceolbert: It was. Your race goes on but it does not change. Rain will not soften it. I believe you would still rather throw a harpoon then sign a parchment.

Thane: I would.

Ceolbert: And you want the old Barn to remain open?

Thane: I do. The children need a place of their own.
(EDGAR enters with helmet. THANE puts it on the ground and stands talking with one foot on it).
The Abbot tells me that there is some parchment which must be signed and witnessed. It is booke–land now, not laen land as it was in Ella's time. I am no scholar and I don't like parchments.

Ceolbert: You have good reasons for your misgivings. Already Paulinus is calling the villagers villeens. Perhaps I shall be able to help you.

Thane: I should like to get it settled and over. Where shall I find your master, the Abbot?

Ceolbert: I expect he is still in the Barn supervising the cleansing. It smells too much of skins and wassailing for their holy clerical nostrils.

Thane: They won't pull it down?

Ceolbert: Heaven forbid! No, they won't pull it down, but they might shut it up and use it exclusively for holy purposes.

Thane: Nothing is holy which is dark!

Ceolbert: Your words cut like a sword, but they ring true.

Thane: (As HILDA turns a somersault). That's right Hilda, do it again.

Ceolbert: But don't let Brother Paulinus see you. He might disapprove and inform the Abbot.

Thane: And what dare the Abbot say to a grandchild of mine?

Ceolbert: I don't know. He came out of a different mould from you, but there's a lot of good in him. He watches the swallows in the Barn, and I believe he could be induced to spare the children their corner if it were not for the sinister legal influence of Brother Paulinus. We must win over the Abbot *before* the parchment is signed.

Thane: You seem to be on our side.

Ceolbert: I am. Your father had two friends. One was Wilred, the other was a wanderer.

Thane: (Looking at him closely) Surely you are not . . . (CEOLBERT coughs and drowns the name).

Ceolbert: I am. I come and I go like the swallows. The Thane of Roxey has more friends in high places than he knows. He is the Grandson of Ella. At times Holy Church goes to sleep, but there are some things which it cannot forget . . . Farewell, we shall meet not many days hence in London. There the word of Uncle Eddy is law. I will take this (the helmet) It might be useful. (Exit CEOLBERT).

Thane: (to children). Do you know who he is?

Freda: Of course we do.

Edgar: We call him Uncle Eddy.

Thane: But you don't know what his rank is!

Ath: Well, anyone can see from his clothes that he is a Benedictine Brother.

Thane: He is not a Brother. He is a Bishop!

All: "A Bishop!" "What!" "No!"

Thane: The second greatest Bishop in all England.

Ath: A Bishop? Why, he is not even an Abbot. He bows to the Abbot and does just as he is told.

Thane: Yes, he knows how to humble himself, but you wait till you see him decked out in all his finery when he comes down to bless the old Barn.

Edgar: I always knew he was a great man.

Freda: He may be a great man but he is one of us.

Smaller Boy: Yes, he is one of us.
(They get into boat and sing).

Row, Thorsmen, row
Freya watches you
The storm clouds are rising
The whales are in view

Row, Thorsmen, throw
The harpoons are out
They cleave through the billows
They stick in his snout.

Row, Thorsmen, row
The sunset is red
The whale is still kicking
But soon he'll be dead.

SCENE II is set in THE MONASTERY OF ALLHALLOWS, BIRKENGE CHIRCHE, LONDON, 8th November, A.D. 845 (St. Paul's having been burnt three years previously).
Three fat and well favoured Saxon Bishops are seated opposite a dish of crabs. Three lean Latin Bishops opposite a pile of manuscripts. The Archbishop's empty seat divides them. A dispute is in progress. The Thane and the Abbot of Roxeth have a table to themselves. Ceolbert Bishop of London is the host.

Ceolbert: No! It must be changed—I will not have it.

Alchun: You must. It is written.

Ceolbert: Then it must be unwritten.

Alchun: Have you no respect for legality? No regard for inflections?

Ceolbert: None when they alter sense. This playing with parchments is nidings work.

Alchun: The spoken and the written word must needs be different. ROXEY is a spoken word. ROXETH a written word.

Ceolbert: And what about 'Seath?'

Alchun: Bishop Ceolbert I have told you that H R O C means Rook, that E.S. implies possession and that SEATH can mean 'a seat,' 'a home,' 'an abode,' 'a spring,' 'a fount,' 'a marsh . . . '

Ceolbert: Or anything else you like to make it mean. SEATH is not a true word. It is not English. It is only half Latin. It is a bastard word and I will not have it.

The Spirit of Roxeth
revisits the Saxon doorway at Allhallows

Alchun: In writing, on parchment, you must.

Ceolbert: I won't.

Tatnoth: Nor will I. Wilred was parish priest of the place for forty years before he became Bishop of Dunwich. He should know. Ask him.

Ceolbert: Ask the learned Abbot! Ask the Thane!

Wilred: Roxey it always has been.

Thane: (emphatically). And ROXEY it must remain.

Alchun: If you insist I will put it in brackets.

Thane: I do insist. (Applause from Saxon end of bench) and I will put you in brackets if you tamper with my possessions.

(Commotion).

Enter GUTHEARD with wand of Office).

Gutheard: Hush! Pray silence for His Grace Ceolnoth of Wessex, Archbishop of Canterbury.

HE retires).

(Enter CROSS BEARER and CEOLBERT and GUTHEARD, followed by CEOLNOTH, ARCHBISHOP of CANTERBURY. Everyone stands. Cross is placed in position. Wand Bearers retire to opposite ends of bench. Archbishop inclines first to bench, then to Abbots table).

Archbishop: Pax vobiscum. From senseless bickerings and from the fury of the Norsemen.

All: Good Lord, deliver us!

Archbishop: (Picking up scroll) So this is the parchment we are to consider.

Alchun: No. That is a new copy of the Rights of Ine.

Ceolbert: I am having it firmly fixed to the Port of London as a reminder and a warning to evil-doers.

Archbishop : Are not these Dooms of Ine a little hard and primitive?

Ceolbert: Yes! But not so hard and primitive as the Norsemen who lit fires in this fair City three years ago and burnt the roof off St. Pauls.

Archbishop: (Lays down MSS). Perhaps you are right. Those crabs look very good.

Tatnoth: Yes! they were brought from Dunwich by Bishop Wilred.

Ceolbert: He has been Parish Priest of Roxey for forty years, and he has worked hard about the transfer of lands to Holy Church.

Wilred: I trust your Grace will accept this rather strange gift.

Archbishop: Indeed I will. What with Salmon from London river, Rooks and Barley from Roxey, and now these crabs from Wilred, we should be graceless if we forgot this happy coming together at Allhallows.

Alchun: These precious parchments from Jarrow are for your Grace's library at Canterbury, when you can return there in safety. Twice they have escaped the fire of the Norsemen.

Archbishop: I shall treasure them, Alchun. Be seated. It is good for brethren from our own dear land, and from overseas where men see things differently, to come together inside the strong walls of London under this thrice blessed roof of Allhallows. There is a wholesome manly bluntless about our host my good friend Bishop Ceolbert. It humbles me to think that I am now sitting in this ancient house of God's Glory, where the Sainted Ertkenwald sat two hundred years ago. Here we are indeed encompassed by a cloud of witnesses. Holy Church must show itself worthy of those witnesses and of its present-day defenders. I rise and salute and welcome to our gathering—WEREMBERT of Roxey—the King's Thane.

Thane: I am a man of few words, but in the name of the folk I rule and the King I serve, I thank you.

Archbishop: It is we who must this day thank you! and through you your ancestors the saintly Wergand and warrior Ella. This is a day in the span of the years which should, in your house and in Roxeth, be long remembered . . . I have been counting heads. Eleven and the Holy Cross. We are now a company of twelve . . . Let us stand . . . and in the Holy silence of Allhallows quietly remember the names of others who have striven in various ways to build up and maintain the good name of Roxeth. (Pause—they sit down again). Pass me the parchment Alchun before the good moment passes. Let me feel it. Yes, it is good durable material. It will last longer than our old bones . . . To your trained eye, Alchun, is the workmanship equally good?

Alchun: Yes, your Grace, but it is not up to the old work of Jarrow.

Humbert: Look at this parchement from Stanes Hulch. It is perfect.

Archbishop: I will examine that Humbert in a still time when there shall be no chiding. No disputings. Proceed Alchun and remember that most of your Auditors have little Latin. When you have finished Ceolbert and Wilred must speak for they are sponsors of this transfer.

Alchun: (Reads from parchment on page 15.) Regnante . . . etc., etc., Hroces Seath . . .

Ceolbert: (Interrupting). Roxey, your Grace. Good old Roxey. Not Roxeth.

Archbishop: Ceolbert—this is no time for bickering. Proceed Alchun.

Alchun: (Continuing with reading). Cum campis y silvis ac pratis.

Archbishop: In a few English words, Ceolbert, that means?

Ceolbert: That good old Roxey is again changing hands.

Wilred: It means that the laen-land which was won so dearly after the bloody Haest on the Hill is being marked with the cross and given over as booke-land to Holy Church.

Archbishop: Have you anything to add Ceolbert?

Ceolbert: Yes I have . . . This helmet was claved from the head of Ludgrin the Dane by that man (points to Thane) when Roxeth, by his strong arm, escaped the fate of London, Rochester and Canterbury. He asks that while he lives, the ancestral village Barn may be used as he and I and Wilred desire.

Archbishop: Is that the wish of the Thane of Roxeth?

Thane: It is.

Archbishop: Do we agree to it?

Bench: (Agrees). We are agreed. Of course. Yes.

Archbishop: Amen! So be it. Do you want a parchment to make it binding?

Thane: No. My word is my bond.

Wilred: His sword is his parchment.

Alchun: See, your Grace, the translation is written here.

Archbishop: Good. How thoughtful of you Alchun.

Alchun: Ceolbert insisted.

Beretred: He would insist.

(Laughter at the Saxon end of the table).

Tatnoth: Uncle Eddy's word is law!

Archbishop: This is no laughing matter. Let Werhard the Abbot read, and Werembert the King's Thane, mark well the words before we set our names and Holy Cross of Christ to it.

Abbot: (Reads) This exchange of land . . . etc., etc., (see Chapter I, Page 10.)

Archbishop: And you think Master Abbot, that this Roxeth is a fair place to have and to hold.

Ceolbert: He should know your Grace. He spends most of his time garping at birds. Counting the rooks' nests; watching the slow flapping herons and listening to the warblers making melody round the haystacks.

Abbot: Roxey, your Grace, has woods full of wild swine. Its red deer come down to my fish ponds to drink. Pike swim in the moat. It has pastures wide, woods and big barns, and in the time of the bluebells when the birds are mating it has such a wealth of treasure that men may see the beauty of heaven from their doorsteps, as they go about their daily tasks.

Archbishop: And what are those tasks Thane Werembert?

Thane: Hunting the wild deer, following the roe, felling the oak trees. Planting the barley and reaping it to fill the barns and the ale horn.

Archbishop: Good. I have heard enough. I will set my name and the Holy Cross of Christ to this parchment, and while the signing and witnessing proceeds, let the choristers sing and the minstrels play.

Elevated Coffin Shrine of Saint Edmund at Pontigny
E. de la Mare Norris.

CHAPTER SEVEN

ST. EDMUND'S POND

A Local History Lesson presented by children of Welldon Park School to their parents on 22nd July, 1946.

On either side of the East window in Sanderstead Parish Church, 14th century wall paintings were recently uncovered. One depicts Saint Edmund the Martyr (840—870) riddled with arrows, the other St. Edmund de Pontigny (1175—1240) wearing his Archbishop's Mitre. We may never know which of these saints gave his name to the old Pond at Roxeth Corner (It was filled in after the Public Health Enquiry of 1849), but as no reference to St. Edmund's Pond has been found prior to the canonisation of Edmund Rich (1246), I like to think that the gentle Archbishop who gave Harrow church its endowment had a personal connection with Roxeth's Pond. Although Edmund Rich inherited St. Augustine's chair and the Harrow Manor from Thomas Becket and like him was exiled to Pontigny, he was quite a different character. St. Richard of Chichester, who attended the elevation of his friends relics at Pontigny, wrote " God had anointed him with the oil of gladness, above all the readers, teachers and disputants of his time." It is therefore interesting to be able to record that though the rich shrine of St. Thomas (Becket) at Canterbury was destroyed by Richard Layton, Rector of Harrow, the shrine of St. Edmunds at Pontigny has survived. By climbing a staircase at the rear of the altar, and looking through the glass side of a coffin, the bones of the saint who gave his name to the pond at Roxeth Corner can still be seen. How beautiful that Pond on Mount Pleasant (the old name for Roxeth Corner) must have been I can guess ; for as a child I spent many hours playing round a similar tree-secluded pond in the quiet gardens of The Grange.

" Calm Soul of all things make it mine
To feel amid the city's jar
That there abides a peace of thine
Man did not make and cannot mar "

THE PLACE throughout is Saint Edmund's Pond.

THE TIME rolls backward from 8th November, A.D. 1945 to 830 and beyond.

EPISODE I

THE SPIRIT OF ROXETH
ROXETH CORNER 1945

CASTE

HEADMISTRESS	MARTIN SHAKESPEARE
BOY SCOUT	BRIAN POTTER
GREEN MONK	ERIC BISHOP

Headmistress I want a Book about Roxeth. Can you direct me to the Kenton Library?

Boy Scout: Yes. Take the 140 bus on the other side of the road. It's just past the Kenton Brook.

Headmistress: I suppose Kenton Brook is the same as the old Lidding Brook.

Boy Scout: They used to think so and they printed it on a map . . . but we know better now.

Headmistress: Indeed and how do you know?

Boy Scout: Well, we scouts should know. We beat the bounds of Roxeth.

Headmistress: You may be right. I must look it up (exit) (Enter a monk dressed in green).

Green Monk: I am a little deaf but did I hear you say ROXETH!?

Boy Scout: You did (Monk prospects with water divining rod).

Green Monk: There's water hereabouts.

Boy Scout: There was. You have struck St. Edmunds Pond.

Green Monk: St. Edmunds Pond? I was trying to find the Lidding Brook. I used to live here eleven hundred years ago and things have changed a little.

Boy Scout: I expect they have.

Green Monk: Do you know where the old Lidding Brook is or where it was?

Boy Scout: All the old roads hereabouts lead to Roxeth Moat and if you go down Shaftesbury Avenue past the Moat you will see the valley through which the old Lidding Brook used to run.

Green Monk: Thanks. A man's best things are nearest him and to the all knowing nothing is lost.

Boy Scout: Nothing is lost!?

Green Monk: Yes. I said 'nothing is lost'. Beyond the Priors orchard and the Lidding Brook I can still see the Herefrethingland marshes and the oak woods and beyond them there is another valley full of white flapping spoonbills.

Boy Scout: Did you say you were 1,100 years old?

Green Monk: No . . . I'm as young and frolicsome as the clouds in the sky. I run for my train in the morning. I flow through the veins of children. I change but I cannot die.

Boy Scout: Who are you?

Green Monk: I am the SPIRIT OF ROXETH . . . Sit down and open your hat. I will show you some of my treasures, (He produces these from a Green bag) A Jacobite Pipe dated 1745, picked up near St. Edmunds Pond, (drops it in Scout Hat) a feather from the hat of the King who lost his head.

Boy Scout: King Charles? (monk nods assent).

Green Monk: A torn parchment dated 1550, relating to St. Edmunds Pond (reads), beaten till their bodies be bloodie.

Boy Scout: What a pretty cap!

Green Monk: Yes, seven hundred years ago it belonged to Valence the page of St. Edmund de Pontigny . . . and what price this? The mitre of St. Thomas of Canterbury (sets it on Scouts head). They killed him and then they worshipped his hat . . . and this (holding up staff) is the most precious of all. I will keep it until it is needed. It withers but it cannot die.You may treasure those other souvenirs.

Boy Scout: Thank you sir. I will put them up in our Patrol Corner.

Green Monk: And each year to keep the memory of Roxeth green you must look out for me at the Boundary Stones.'

Boy Scout: We will.

EPISODE II

THE ENQUIRY OF 1849

CASTE

After a good lunch at the King's Head the Public Health Commission arrives at the pond.

Dr. Hewlett: Our present knowledge suggests that cholera rises from low pestilential places like this.

C. T. Clark: Have you had any cases of cholera at the school?

Dr. Hewlett: No. But the pond should be filled in.

C. T. Clark: Does it serve any useful purpose?

R. B. Chapman: In winter they use it for horse washing.

Dr. Hewlett: In summer as you see it is too filthy even for that.

C. T. Clark: Where do the cottages get their water?

R. B. Chapman: From a ten foot well in William Martin's garden. Would you like to see it?

C. T. Clark: Yes. (William Martin the pig killer who had been watching from his garden gate stopped sharpening his knife, wiped his fingers and touched his hat; but what he said and what he thought of that official enquiry of 1849 is not recorded in the minutes)

EPISODE III

THE SEXTON AND THE FARRIER 1745

CASTE

GILBERT FISHER	FRANCES BARRS
JOCK NOBES	ANGELA STAPLES

After several attempts to light his clay from his flint Gilbert Fisher the sexton sits back and listens to the nightingales till he falls asleep. A Green Monk—" The Spirit of Roxeth " emerges from the pond, takes Gilbert's pipe and disappears. Enter Jock Nobes the farrier with two tankards of cider. They drink.

Gilbert: Thanks Jock. They nightingales be singing mighty fine Tonight. Baint they?

Jock: I can't say that I takes much notice of them myself... but my old missus likes em . . . I see the swifts be still circling round the Barn.

Gilbert: Yes they will be circling round the Barn and dipping at the Pond long after you and I are gone.

Jock: The water in the old Pond is very low this summer.

Gilbert: Well what can you expect with this weather... Any news at your forge of those mad marching Scotsmen?

Jock: They've no turned back. So perhaps we shall be hearing the skirl of their bagpipes before you put on your Sunday suit.

EPISODE IV

KING CHARLES AND THE ROUNDHEADS
27th APRIL, 1646

CASTE

ROUNDHEAD OFFICER	BARBARA THOMPSON
JEREMIAH MINTON	FRANCES BARTLETT
KING CHARLES	SHEILA CHRISTELOW
SERVANT	EVELYN LIGHT

Roundhead Officer: Jeremiah Minton?

Jeremiah: Coming Sir . . . Yes sir!

Roundhead Officer: Do you recognise any of those three horsemen galloping up Northolt Road?

Jeremiah: No sir. I can't say as I do. They be all foreigners to these parts. Shall I mount and follow en?

Roundhead Officer: No get up that ladder and watch them from the Barn. They are sure to stop at St. Edmund's' Pond.

King Charles: Shall we dismount at the Pond?

Servant: No sire... we are being watched . . . we shall be challenged if we halt . . .

Jeremiah: (from the ladder) They have not stopped at the Pond.

Roundhead Officer: Which road are they taking?

Jeremiah:	The middle one.
Roundhead Officer:	That's all right. Come down. They must be friends of Sir Gilbert Gerrard . . . What are you garping at now?
Jeremiah:	I don't know . . . but there's an old monk dressed in green by the Pond . . . He is picking up something white.
Roundhead Officer:	Now don't you tell me you have seen the Spirit of Roxeth or I shall have to cut down your cider ration.
Jeremiah:	Well, he is still there. (officer goes up ladder).
Roundhead Officer:	Yes I can . . . but he's not real . . . I can see through him . . . What do you make of it?
Jeremiah:	I don't make nothing of it . . . but Betty Cox and the old folks say it does not pay to go against the Spirit of old Roxeth.
Roundhead Officer:	Nonsense! Get your horse. Take your gun and follow those horsemen.

EPISODE V

THE STEWARD AND THE TYTHING MAN, 1550

STEWARD	MOLLY BALDING
MONK	GORDON BREEZE
NICHOLAS	DORETHY HARDWICK
HENRI BETTE	JANET RANSLEY

A monk is arranging the Manor Court; Tything man watches. Enter Steward. Monk hands him parchment. He reads it.

Steward:	Let them both be beaten for an hour at the post till their bodies be bloodie . . . Will they never learn that all the fish in the Pond belong to the Manor . . . and if they talk about St. Edmund's bounty let them be beaten again and each day for a week.
Monk:	Yes my Lord.
Steward:	And what are you doing in the Court, Nicholas Horstrappere?
Nicholas:	An it please you my Lord I speak for Robert Edlin of Dobbs Tything in that Henri Bette of the Ermitage is not stoppinge the muck and water flowing from St. Edmund's Pond. It is a nuisance to the whole tything.
Steward:	Let Henri Bette be called.
Monk:	(calls) Henri Bette (he enters).
Henri Bette:	Yes sire.
Steward:	Am not I his Lordships' Steward?
Henri Bette:	Yes sire (correcting himself) Yes my Lord.
Steward:	And have I not ordered you to safeguard my Lord's waste all along the Roxeth verge?

Henri Bette:	Yes my Lord.
Steward:	Then see to it . . . lest worse befall you!
Henri Bette:	Yes my Lord (backs out).
Steward:	And Nicholas . . .
Nicholas:	Yes sire.
Steward:	When you call at The Grange for your victuals and cider see that these matters are duly recorded. (Exit. Nicholas, talks to the monk who continues writing Exeunt . . . Enter The Spirit of Roxeth. He tears the whipping parchment in two and puts it in his bag with other treasures)

EPISODE VI

THE ARCHBISHOP AND THE RECTOR

1240

VALENCE, *the Page*	J. GREAGSBY
MONK	D. HUGHES
EDMUND DE PONTIGNY	F. BARTLETT
ELIAS DE DERHAM	C. BOYCE

A Benedictine monk is fishing at the pond. Enter Valence the Page.

Valence:	Have you caught anything?
Monk:	Yes some fine lamphreys for your master the Archbishop. I hope he enjoys them. He works too hard and eats too little.
Valence:	But you like him?
Monk:	Everyone likes him. Edmund Rich is the best landlord and the best Archbishop . . .
Valence:	Softly! Here he comes.
Monk:	I wonder what Master Elias de Dereham is begging for now . . . a new church or a new rectory.
Valence:	Neither. He is begging for a new roof and a new steeple. (Enter Archbishop Edmund, Rector Elias de Dereham, Richard of Chichester and others).
Edmund:	It will need a lot of money. How many tythings are there in Roxeth?
Elias:	Three, Newton, Dobbs and Heath.
Edmund:	And how many in Wembra Lea?
Elias:	One, your Grace.
Edmund:	Good. Now read me that list of tithed things that are offered at our altar of St. Mary.
Elias:	(reads) Cheese, butter, milk : lambs and wool ; calves, little pigs and goats ; chicken and bees.
Edmund:	Is that from my land or from the Parish?
Elias:	From both. There are now as many hives in the Parish as there were bees five years ago.
Edmund:	Good.

Copy of Original Design For Clerestory Window, St. Mary's, Harrow
(*By* T. F. Curtis)

Becket To Abbot Simon, 17th December, 1170
" This Abbot has done more for me than all my suffragans "

(*Engraved by* THOMAS BARBER, 1879 . . . IN HIS 81ST YEAR)

ROXETH GRANGE

Is this on the site of the Archbishops "Granga et Capella"?

Elias: There is also the tithe of the pannage, the garden produce and the hay. We must not forget the hay . . . and you remember there is the Vicar's Christmas offering to me of fifty geese.

Edmund: Yes I remember. You feasted my guests and my men royally Master Elias. Can we complete the list now and dispatch it?

Elias: No my lord. Not till Hamo comes. The Roxeth hay tithe is the biggest of all.

Edmund: (calls) Valence!

Valence: (bows with flourish of cap), Yes, my Lord.

Edmund: You can leave these parchments with Hugh Calne the Bailiff. The rest may go but bid them bolt the outer curtilage gate (Valence helps Monk carry fishing tackle and drops his cap. All except Edmund and Elias quietly withdraw) (to Elias), It is a warm evening . . . we will sit out here in the shade till Hamo comes from his sweating hayfields . . . To spend a quiet hour watching the changing shadows on this pond is not a waste of time. Sit you there Master Elias and pattern out your steeple. (Elias sketches, Blackbird sings, St. Edmund de Pontigny closes his eyes and listens while the SPIRIT of ROXETH gathers the page's cap into his sack. Edmund looks at the sketch of the steeple).

CURTAIN

BECKET'S WRATH
17th DECEMBER, 1170
CASTE

THOMAS, *Archbishop of Canterbury*	D. BARTLETT
SIMON, ABBOT *of St. Albans*	M. SHAKESPEARE
GUNTER	B. POTTER
SERVANT	G. BREEZE

A party of monks and ecclesiastics arrive at the Pond. It is the retinue of Archbishop Thomas (Becket) who is accompanied by Simon, Abbot of St. Albans.

Thomas: The wind blows cold. The snow is deep.

Simon: It's warmer in the Grange. Why not turn back and rest till you can come to see our cradle play in the safe warmth of Albans sacred shrine?

Thomas: No, Simon; by the divine decree it has been ordered otherwise. I have outstayed my time and this white frozen pond must mark the parting of our ways.

Simon: I had hoped . . .

Thomas: Do not tempt me Simon. The path that I must take leads up this hill through frozen lanes . . . and cheering crowds . . . .to ageless Canterbury

Simon: You will not be persuaded.

Thomas: No. I see how things will end. God's common people trust me. The skies grow red. The flame laps up the candle.

Simon: You are too old, too weak, to carry on this dog fight with the king.

Thomas: The Church is old; but never weak. Why did I sign that wretched document? The easy way is good but never right. England must steam before she breaks her icy shackles. Forgive me Simon . . . and though you cannot follow me up this hill. God bless you still my dear old friend. (They embrace, Simon and his monks return to the Grange) Gunter!

Gunter: Yes, sire.

Thomas: Mark well the way that Abbot Simon goes and in the days that come remember, He helped me more than all my suffragans (Noise of brawling). What's wrong?

Gunter: I'll go and see (Exit Gunter: he returns rather agitated) De Broc and other well armed men are coming down the hill. You must retire into the Grange. Its walls are strong. They are wreaking vengance on your mules.

Thomas: Is Nigel Sackville with them?

Gunter: Yes and other men who say they serve the King.

Thomas: They serve their own proud lusts.

Gunter: Come away (Servants hurry past including one with the Archbishop's crozier, another leading a mutilated mule).

Thomas: So my best mule is maimed by those that eat my corn.

Gunter: Come away my Lord, (pulls at him.)

Thomas: No. Fetch back my crozier. The undying church stands fast. I will not leave this frozen pond, for I have vowed to break their ill used power, though twenty puppet kings should come between (Gunter hurries off and returns with the crozier).

Thomas: Thanks. My arm grows weak. Time was when I could take and give a cudgelling (Pause, a winter robin breaks the silence. Becket stares in the pond).

Servant: They have turned back

Thomas: And I am glad. I saw the Towers of Canterbury reflected in this ice. Ride on . . . To Canterbury. Nothing can stop us now.

Tableau—The Canterbury Pilgrims

EPISODE VIII
CHAUCER VISITS THE GRANGE
1380

CHAUCER
LADY IDONEA BREMBRE
GILBERT, *son of Nicholas Brembre*

Chaucer is walking by the Pond with Lady Idonea wife of Sir Nicholas Brembre.

Chaucer: What a grand old Pond.

Lady Idonea:	Yes. It's proper name is Becket's Wrath but the Roxeth folk will call it St. Edmund's Pond I cannot stop them. Did you enjoy your latest pilgrimage? Nicholas told me about your romance with the wife of Bath. He thought it very funny.
Chaucer:	Yes I enjoyed it all, especially the company. They came from every shire of England . . . In the flesh this Becket must have been a powerful fellow. Now you cannot see his shrine. It is heaped high with jewels.
Lady Idonea:	(to hound), Down Roger.
Chaucer:	What a beautiful pattern these hawthorn petals make along the path.
Lady Idonea:	I wish you could get Nicholas to think so. He is never at home. His head is stuffed full of plottings and business. Will you shew us some more of those beautiful coloured manuscripts Master Chaucer.
Gilbert, Son of Nicholas:	No. He has promised to come with us to Dobbs Mill and if he does not come quickly father will be taking him off to Downe again.

EPISODE IX
GEOFFREY DE MANDEVILLE
1070

Geoffrey de Mandeville:	Take my horse and Eleanor's palfrey through the wicket and water them at the Priest fish pond.
Servant:	Not at the Moat?
Geoffrey de Mandeville:	No, the steward is an upstart. He grudges me my holding on the Mount. He is no friend of mine: but make no disputinge for his master the Archbishop hath the ear of my Lord King.

EPISODE X
THE BROTHERS OF ROXETH
A.D. 830

ABBOT WERHARD, *The Green Monk*	E. BISHOP
CEOLFRITH	D. NORMAN
PAULINUS	M. SHAKESPEARE
WILRED	W. WOODS
HUNBERT	G. BREEZE
BENEDICTINE MONKS ..	B. POTTER, D. BARTLETT, A. HOWLETT

Abbot Werhard (..The Spirit of Roxeth) seated on an abbot's chair is gazing into the waters of the Pond. He holds a Glastonbury staff. Chanting Benedictines are heard in the distance.

"Honour, and blessing and glory, wisdom, power and might,
Be unto HIM who has loved us and called us to carry his light."

They are returning after many years of exile to Roxeth—a burnt out hamlet which only Wilred can remember.

" We are the brothers of Roxeth. We sing of the days that are past, of tythings, hamlet, and manor of Bonefield battle and blast."

Paulinus has assumed the roll of leader. He follows close on the Cross Bearer. The others are marching and singing in pairs. Wilred leaning heavily on a young monk who carries a bow. Werhard goes to meet them.

Ceolfrith: (Kneels and hands the Cross to Werhard who blesses each monk as he passes). Hail Werhard!

Paulinus: Hail Abbot Werhard. Prepotens in Anglia!

Werhard: Welcome back to Roxeth. It is a long time since these sad groves last heard the voices of the chanting Benedictines.

Wilred: Over 30 years my Lord.

Werhard: Is it so long? I will chant another verse while you rest by this peaceful pond. Maybe the birds will take our reunion chorus up to the highest heaven. They have been very faithful to me and to this pond. But how tired you look Wilred!

Wilred: I am.

Paulinus: Yes it is a long weary way across those Herefrethingland marshes.

Wilred: Every step was heaven till I saw this burnt out village.

Hunbert: And I think we lost our way.

Wilred: No we did not, my Lord ; but the old paths are sadly overgrown and some of the praying stones have been taken away.

Werhard: We must restore them.

Wilred: We will.

Werhard: Fetch my chair . . . Now fetch my staff. It was cut from the Holy Thorn at Glastonbury, Ella's father gave it to me. It withers but it cannot die (leading Wilred to the Abbot's chair). Sit down Wilred.

Wilred: No . . . my . . . not in your seat.

Werhard: Yes, Wilred you must, and take this staff. It will strengthen you.

Wilred: I am a tired old man. Surely you are not going away.

Werhard: I am. I must. Canterbury needs me as Roxeth needs you. One day your burnt up Roxeth will have more people in it than my Canterbury. This is another day of beginnings for you and for all of us. Roxeth is trampled down but it will rise again.

Wilred: It must.

Werhard: Sit back and rest . . .

Paulinus: As we came by Pilhead's house I noticed that it was hardly damaged. It would be warm and comfortable in winter. There are possibilities in this place if we could get some labour to build it up; and this old pond could be cleaned out improved and stocked with fish.

Werhard: You would not frighten the birds away Paulinus?

Paulinus: Well at least we should be sure of our fish.

Werhard: And what do you think Wilred?

Wilred: The Thane's house is too comfortable and other tasks await us.

Hunbert: Wilred is right, let us be content with Offa's tiny chapel till we can bring Stidbert's altar back from Hayes.

Wilred: How can we be comfortable while others suffer. First we must help the villagers rebuild their cottages. Then we must deepen the Roxbourne and keep the old path across the marshes open. We must grow food.

Werhard: We must make our lives our chapel. To labour is to pray and by working together we shall become the Friends and the Brothers of Roxeth.

Wilred: That's it. We are the " Brothers of Roxeth."

(As they sing their Benedictine chant shadows of eleven centuries rise from St. Edmunds Pond for the concluding Tableau).

Tune " The Carpenters Bench."

Monks:
We are the Brothers of Roxeth
We sing of the days that are past,
Of tythings, hamlet, and manor
Of Bonefield, battle and blast.

Werhard:
When Roxeth was cinders and ashes
After the first Danish raid,
We stood by the women and children
And built up the old stockade.

Monks:
We are the Brothers of Roxeth
We march down the ages as one.
We rise from the Smoke of the ash heap
Like Phoenix to worship the Sun.

Werhard:
Some men were King's advisers
Others were hewers of wood
Becket and Lanfranc were mighty
Anselm and Edmund were good.

Monks:
We are the Brothers of Roxeth
A parchment gives us a name
And all that dwell in our borders
Shall share in our ancient fame.

All:
Blessing and honour and glory
Wisdom, power and might
Be unto HIM who has loved us
And called us to carry HIS light.

CHAPTER EIGHT

THE BIRDS OF ROXETH

The Elimination of Beauty.

(1900—1948)

THERE have been many changes in human and bird population since men first found their feet and came down from the tree-tops and birds first found their wings and soared above them ; but possibly none more drastic than those which have taken place round London during the present century.

The face of Roxeth has changed. Its lanes, its trees, its birds have gone ; and to compensate for its loss of open spaces, sunlight, natural food and natural beauty, its children have electric light, orange juice and cinemas. Roxeth is no longer its old self : it is absorbed into London, and the changes from fields towards slums are called progress.

My earliest memories of Roxeth are of apple trees and huntsmen, birds and snow. Many birds, and much snow. There were times when the twelve farms, the marshes, the lanes and the orchards between Roxeth and Ruislip were covered to a depth of four feet and only the elms and tallest hawthorn hedges then stood out above the snow.

They were sad times for the poor. The parochial soup kitchens were kept busy. The gulls were tempted to visit London. That was their first taste of London's " fine large sprats " and the beginning of London's annual white invasion. It was a sad time for the birds ; but worse times were to follow, for most of the countryside between Roxeth marshes and Ruislip Reservior is now buried under a thirty foot fall of suburban bricks and mortar, which does not melt.

The elms, stunted oaks, willows and hawthorn hedges which linked man to the birds are gone. 'You cannot stir a flower without troubling a star,' nor lay waste the green things of the earth without hurting birds and man.

Between 1900 and 1910 I made the acquaintance of Harold Park, a boy from Cumberland. He taught me not only how to blow eggs with one hole and market them to boys of the Top School but how to distinguish between the whinchat and the stonechat, between the winter butcher bird—a great grey shrike who visited the top of a crab apple tree at the bottom of the Long Mile—and the red-backed shrike who made butchers' shops on the spiky hawthorns of Naylor's field.

Our blackberrying expeditions took us along tangled lanes full of gipsies and bird catchers, past orchards where there were wrynecks, bullfinches and hawfinches and into Mr. Rayners private garden at Dabbs Hill, where a pied flycatcher built in a nesting box on the island in the centre of the pond. Early morning expeditions emptying mole traps took us in the opposite direction through small fields with ponds full of fluffy baby moorhens to an overhanging willow (now replaced by No. 47 Park Lane) in which a cuckoo had deposited its egg in the restricted space which held a wagtails nest. Beyond the small fields were the marshes, where we listened to corncrakes and water rails, set up snipe, and watched redshanks and golden plover feeding. In the evening thousands of rooks flew across the marshes " on their way home from school " and at sundown a solitary heron would sail sedately across the sky from Zion House towards Ruislip Reservoir. Old residents said there was once a small heronry near the ancient mulberry tree in the Northolt Rectory garden.

During the winter holidays we concealed ourselves in Mr. Temple's pigsties (now No. 15 Eastcote Lane) and caught birds under a sieve poised on a dung heap. After measuring them from nose tip to tail tip we let them go. In this way meadow pipits, redwings, wagtails, and dunnocks came into my land.

About 1904 after my friend's three brothers had returned from the Boer War we used to take tea and American cream soda to the volunteers in the Shooting Butts fields. It was then I first became interested in the autumn manoevres of an army corps of peewits who assembled to drill on this wide open space (now Roxbourne Ward, one of London's most solid suburbs) as if for some important campaign. The assembly continued year after year until every inch of their vast parade ground was built over.

As the century grew older, we sometimes went on foot along the Harrow Road (then a country lane as far as Willesden) to the South Kensington Museum to identify our rarer findings. They included the egg of a woodchat shrike, whose soiled nest, after the young had flown, I preserved for many years.

From 1910—1914 I was so busy studying that I hardly noticed the encroachments made on the haunts of my boyhood by three new railways and many new houses. First the plovers' nesting fields were converted into ' pleasure grounds ' ; then Naylor's nurseries, a paradise for shrikes, hawfinches, wrynecks, warblers, tits and owls, were sold up. Then one of Roxeth's twenty rookeries dwindled because it was constantly let for circuses ; finally even Temple's farm buildings, orchards and pigsties were replaced by suburban dwellings. Barnett's big field, in which the huntsmen assembled, was cut up and now contains 507 houses, 59 shops, a cinema and a school.

BIRDS OF THE ROXETH TO RUISLIP AREA
1925 - 1927
CLASSIFIED BY THEIR MOST FAVOURED HABITAT

(*The number gives the total number of times recorded out of a possible* 40)

	Roxeth Marshes		Roxeth Fields		Eastcote Village		Ruislip Woods		Ruislip Reservoir	
Residents	Reed Bunting	9	Lapwing	29	Starling	40	Woodpigeon	22	Coot	34
			Hedge Sparrow	26	House Sparrow	39	Pheasant	16	Moorhen	25
			Skylark	23	Rook	39	Partridge	14	Great Crested Grebe	21
			Meadow Pipit	19	Robin	39	Jay	12	Swan	19
			Carrion Crow	7	Song Thrush	37	Missel Thrush	10	Mallard	18
			Kestrel	7	Chaffinch	37	Sparrow Hawk	9	Dabchick	17
			Goldfinch	7	Blackbird	36	Longtailed Tit	9		
			Tree Sparrow	5	Blue Tit	30	Marsh Tit	6		
			Whinchat	5	Great Tit	30	Magpie	4		
			Stonechat	4	Wren	27	Tawny Owl	4		
			Yellow Hammer	4	Jackdaw	25	Green Woodpecker	3		
			Linnet	3	Pied Wagtail	22	Bullfinch	3		
					Cole Tit	7				
					Greenfinch	6				
					Treecreeper	3				
					Barn Owl	3				
					Nuthatch	2				
					Greater Spotted Woodpecker	1				
Summer Visitors	Sedge Warbler	4	Whitethroat	7	Swallow	19	Willow Warbler	11	Reed Warbler	1
	Yellow Wagtail	2	Cuckoo	6	Martin	18	Goldcrest	2	Kingfisher	4
	Wheatear	2	Lesser Whitethroat	4	Swift	11	Nightingale	1	Sand Martin	1
	Grey Wagtail	1	Red Backed Shrike	1	Chiffchaff	6	Woodwren	1		
			Tree Pipit	1	Blackcap	3	Turtle Dove	1		
			Golden Orcole	1	Spotted Flycatcher	1				
					Hawfinch	1				
					Garden Warbler	1				
Winter Visitors	Snipe	5	Redwing	14	Siskin	1			Tufted Duck	15
	Blackheaded Gull	4	Fieldfare	13					Pochard	13
	Herring Gull	1	Golden Plover	2					Heron	7
	Redshank	3							Teal	3
									Brent Geese	2
									Barnicle Goose	1
									Widgeon	1

1914—1918

I spent on active service and though I kept records of birds in Picardy, Salonica and Sinai, my thoughts often went back to the open spaces, the barns and the lanes of Roxeth. On my return I watched parts of England which I regarded as peculiarly my own being eaten up by something worse than Sinai locusts. Without a thought of green belts, open spaces, bird sanctuaries or the needs of growing children, Roxeth's three great tythings were being developed. Brooks were cleaned and buried, hedges cut down, and trees felled apparently on the assumption that everything green was unnecessary or unsanitary. The open drain, a route for kingfishers from Ruislip to Harrow Park, was sealed and reserved for rats. Except at Bury Street, Ruislip, all the new concrete roads were cut and left as naked scars on the landscape. Realising that trees are a necessary link between man and his ally, the bird, I joined the Royal Society for the Protection of Birds. Education, as promoted by the R.S.P.B. " Bird and Tree Scheme " and Junior Bird Recorders Club, is doing more than legislation to preserve beauty in Surburbia.

1925—1930

On 1st January, 1925, to give a group of lads just leaving school an interest in life, we began the 12th HARROW SCOUTS' BIRD SURVEY. Each Sunday morning armed with field glasses and plaster-of-paris for taking caste of birds' footprints we made our way, via the Sewer Farm and the Shooting Butts, through Eastcote Village to Ruislip Woods and Ruislip Reservior. The findings and more tangible results of this survey were listed and recorded on a large scale map, but the joy of those long hours in sunshine, snow and rain cannot be expressed on paper. I shall never forget the exclamation, " What is this big yellow bird with blood on its beak? " It proved to be a golden oriole. It was in a field down the Long Mile, where St. Andrew's Church now stands. It is good to spot rare birds in out-of-the-way places, and our list slowly rose from one to eighty-nine species ; but there is a still greater joy in meeting and being at home with old friends in familiar surroundings. To outsiders, our map was an ornithological record ; to us it was honeycombed with memories of individual birds whom we met week after week and whom we learned to know and love. It was for this reason we were content to go the same ramble week after week. We continued our observations even in bad weather, and were rewarded by bird track puzzles in the snow, by the sight of geese in flight, and the joy of finding that our redwings had returned to their same hawthorn hedge.

In March, April and May, before the hedges grew thick with leaves or the woods with bracken, we were able to sort out the chiff-chaff from the willow warbler, the lesser from the greater whitethroat and linnets and bunting from pipits and sparrows. As the hedges darkened and the air filled with dazzling sunshine, we learned together that posture, flight and song were surer guides to recognising our friends than the colours and markings of the textbooks ; but the surest guide as the following list shows, was 'habitat.' Each of the five habitats had its particular birds and the chaffinch was the only bird which nested in all five.

Chaffinches have probably nested in our neighbourhood even longer than our ancestral rooks. They are ancient residents and they may have sung in the birch woods that sprung up round the Hill just after the ice age.

Where did you come from chaffinch dear,
Into this smoke–ridden atmosphere?
Did you watch the Ice age disappear
As you sang from your birch tree ever so clear?
Did you welcome the oakwoods and then the farms
And add to each a share of your charms?
  Sing on. Sing on. It is suburbs now
But the chaffinch sings from the avenue bough.

1. AT THE MARSHES we scared up snipe, made plaster casts, got on speaking terms with a gipsy's tame jackdaw, and watched rooks, rats, jackdaws, gulls, starlings and boys digging for treasure in the corporation dust heap.

2. THE SHOOTING BUTTS FIELDS. Between Roxeth marshes and Eastcote Village there were two miles of fields unbroken by roads or houses. Here we listened to skylarks, tried to estimate the number of meadow pipits, and visited a certain gatepost to hold postmortems on the remains of the sparrow hawks supper (greenfinch in summer and fieldfare in winter).

3. EASTCOTE VILLAGE was a bird sanctuary and as we stopped to count the tits, nuthatches or goldcrests on Mr. Joce's monkey puzzle tree, we could hear blackcaps singing and woodpeckers drumming.

4. RUISLIP WOODS were preserved for game from the days of Cassivelaunus. They are now open to the public ; but the number of jays, owls, hawks and magpies is not so great as when they were shot and hung up on gamekeepers gibbets ; nor is the early morning volume of song as loud as when we camped there in 1924, 1925 and 1926.

5. RUISLIP RESERVIOR is now a Lido. Here in the winter we could be sure of seeing jack snipe and woodcock and several of the less common ducks and geese. Brent and Barnicle geese disappear from our records on 25th January, 1925. In the summer from a hide, we watched the breeding ceremonial of the redbacked shrikes and the great crested grebes, and listened to the grasshopper warblers reeling until the rooks went home and the nightjars began churring. They were happy days and I should like to see the odd distant unwanted corner of Ruislip Reservoir preserved for birds, insects, plants and naturalists; but beauty passes, however fair it be, and when I crumble who will remember the birds that once nested round Ruislip Lido?

1927
THE CASE OF ROOK VERSUS GULL

In January, 1927 when snow was on the ground I watched a battle being fought out across the Roxeth marshes between the local rooks and hordes of invading gulls. The resident rooks had been in possession of their 'Hroces-Seath' territory for over a thousand years. They had watched history being made ; but the oldest dynasties come to an end, and I realised that I was standing at a turn of the tide. Wave after wave of white invaders bore down upon the small black phalanx of rooks and drove them back from the ashheap, back from the marshes into their ancestral trees—the boundary elms. There the black rooks rallied. They resumed the attack. They were only a fraction of their former fighting strength (man's progress had thinned the rookeries), but they fought on : and it was three quarters of an hour before they were finally driven from their ancient feeding grounds.

My sympathy was entirely with the losers ; but I have taken kindly to the usurping blackheaded gulls who came from the Baltic, and I am glad I kept notes of their mighty invasion of Middlesex. London's winter sky would now be grey and desolate without them. I have had over three hundred of them in my hands, and they carry my numbered rings backwards and forwards across the North Sea, staining them yellow in the Baltic marshes. The old order changeth yielding place to new, but perhaps even yet we have not heard the last of the Roxeth rooks.

1930—1945
BIRDS IN A ROXETH GARDEN

By 1930 there were no field paths, and few fields, left between Roxeth and Ruislip ; so I decided to encourage the birds to visit my garden. In size and shape, but nothing else, No. 91 resembles the other ninety gardens in Woodend Avenue. My scouts were finding it difficult to make a collection of leaves of the commoner English trees, so I planted acorns, conkers and slippings from the commoner English trees in my garden ; and in the centre I set a furze bush. A cock stonechat at once took possession of this, and for nine years he remained the most regular resident of the garden. A hen joined him each summer. In 1937 and 1938 they brought their youngsters into the gorse bush for safety and shelter while they fed them, and in 1940 they built within five yards of the garden fence. In 1930 three cuckoos lived within earshot. Only one has survived. In 1938 our last nightingale moved from old Bowden House nearer into the built-up area and nightly entertained the residents of Woodend ; but in the winter of the same year the elms which gave him some seclusion were cut down and he has not returned. A tawny owl and a common gull now rest on the white poplar tree that has grown up since the rooks departed. Hedge accentors and blackbirds still nest in my garden, and blue tits in the lamp post on the adjoining railway bridge, Goldfinches still come each autumn to the railway bank to empty the thistle pods, and more than once a willow warbler has picked his way round the rockery. Altogether fifty-two species of birds including four Bewick swans and an Arctic Skua have settled in or passed over my Roxeth garden.

Like our native Roxeth rooks, other useful and beautiful birds would like to come back home if individuals and corporate bodies gave them appropriate encouragement. Like our children, birds need space to exercise, more greenstuff, more sunlight and more fresh air. That is one of the many reasons why Friends of Roxeth have asked the Harrow Urban District Council to preserve two historic fields in the heart of this old parish.

The following is a list of some of the birds which have visited the garden or the immediate neighbourhood of 91 Woodend Avenue, Roxeth since September, 1930.

Carrion crow, rook, jackdaw, starling, greenfinch, goldfinch, linnet, chaffinch, house sparrow, skylark, meadow pipit, pied wagtail, great tit, blue tit, coal tit, marsh tit, long tailed tit, spotted flycatcher, chiff-chaff, willow warbler, whitethroat, lesser white-throat, fieldfare, missel thrush, song thrush, redwing, blackbird, stonechat, robin, hedge sparrow, wren, swallow, house martin, swift, great spotted woodpecker, cuckoo, tawny owl, little owl, kestrel, heron, Bewick swans, mallard, woodpigeon, stock dove snipe, lapwing, black headed gull, common gull, herring gull, lesser black backed gull, Arctic skua and partridge.

A LIST OF BIRDS

I have observed between ROXETH and RUISLIP during the present century.

A. .seen during the period 1900—1924
B. .seen during the period 1925—1927 (figures give number of times recorded out of a possible 40).
C. .seen during the period 1928—1942 (figures give number of times recorded in 1941—1942 out of a possible 15).
D. .seen since 1942.

Where the letter denoting the period appears in *italic* this indicates that the species has become restricted to the Ruislip area. Total 128. Of these 90 have nested in the district and the 9 species underlined should be regarded as rare visitors. The decrease in passerines was largely due to the spread of suburbia ; the increase in gulls, waterfowl, and waders, to an increased use by these birds of artificial reservoirs. A picture of the Bird life of old Roxeth can best be formed by a present day visit to Ruislip.

Carrion Crow—A ; B, 7 ; C, 15 ; D. Has bred continuously near Stroud Gate. Survives in Suburbia better than the Rook. Increasing at Ruislip Lido.

Rook—A ; B, 39 ; C, 15 ; D. After a short revival noted by T. A. Harrisson in 1931, has steadily decreased.

Jackdaw—A ; B, 25 ; C, 6 ; D. Has ceased to breed in the Railway Arches.
Magpie—A ; B, 4 ; C, 1 ; *D.*
Jay—A ; B, 12 ; C, 5 ; D.
Starling—A ; B, 40 ; C, 15 ; D.
Golden Oriole—B, 1 ; 25/10/15. Male watched opposite Dobbs Hill Estate by T. L. Bartlett, R. Cutmore, A. Rook, L. Horne.
Hawfinch—A ; – ; – ; *D.* Used to breed at St. Hilda's and Temples Orchard.
Greenfinch—A ; B, 6 ; – ; D.
Goldfinch—A ; B, 17 ; C, 2 ; D.
Siskin—A ; B, 2 ; C, 1 ; D. Regular at Frays River. Less regular Eastcote.
Mealy Redpoll—A. Winter visitor.
Lesser Redpoll—A ; B ; – ; *D.*
Twite—A. Winter visitor. Trapped by H. Park.
Linnet—A ; B, 3 ; C, 1 ; D.
Bullfinch—A ; B, 4 ; – ; – ; Formerly widespread. Now local Ruislip.
Chaffinch—A ; B, 37 ; C, 13 ; D. A hardy survivor in the suburbs.
Brambling—A ; B, 1 ; – ; D. Recent records just outside area at Kenton and Ickenham.
Corn Bunting—A. Rifle Range Fields.
Yellow Hammer—A ; B, 4 ; C, 4 ; *D.* Formerly widespread. Now Ruislip.
Reed Bunting—A ; B, 9 ; C, 8 ; *D.* Formerly resident at Newton S.F.
Snow Bunting—D 14/11/28. South Hill Avenue. T.L.B. and D.A.W.
House Sparrow—A ; B, 39 ; C. 15 ; D.
Tree Sparrow—A ; B, 5 ; C, 5 ; D. Formerly common resident. Several colonies near Roxeth Ashheap. Now rare.
Skylark—A ; B, 23 ; C, 8 ; D. Formerly widely distributed. Now Field End and Ruislip.
Tree Pipit—A ; B ; C, 5 ; *D.* Bred in built-up area Roxbourne till 1925, and at Ruislip till 1944.
Meadow Pipit—A ; B, 19 ; C. 6 ; D. Formerly abundant at Shooting Butts Fields.
Yellow Wagtail—A ; B, 2 ; – ; –. Regular visitor to Newton S.F. till 1930.
Grey Wagtail—A ; B, 1 ; – ; –. Occasional visitor to Newton S.F.
Pied Wagtail—A ; B, 22 ; C, 6 ; D.
Tree-Creeper—A ; B, 3 ; – ; D. Local at Mount Park.
Nuthatch—A ; B, 2 ; – ; D. Local at Mount Park. Bred 1947.
Great Tit—A ; B. 30 ; C, 12 ; D.
Blue Tit—A ; B, 30 ; C, 15 ; D. Breeds regularly in suburban lamp posts.

Coal Tit—A ; B, 7 ; C, 2 ; –.
Marsh Tit—A ; B, 6 ; C ; D. Mount Park, Eastcote, Ruislip.
Willow Tit— – – C ; *D*. Local to Ruislip Common side of Reservoir.
Long-tailed Tit—A ; B, 9 ; C, 4 ; D.
Great Grey Shrike—A ; – ; C ; D. Seen both at Northolt and Roxeth at beginning of century. One returned each winter 1905 to 1908 to Crab Apple Trees at bottom of Long Mile. It reappeared in this locality from 27th January to 8th February, 1945. Another bird wintered on Ruislip Common in 1939—1940.
Red Backed Shrike—A ; B, 1 ; C, 3 ; D. Bred regularly at Roxeth up to 1914. Still breeds in definite territories at Ruislip.
Woodchat Shrike—A. Nested successfully along roadside near Northolt 1908. Cock bird and young seen and nest with addled egg retained by me for several years.
Waxwing—D. Many records Roxeth, Eastcote and all parts of Harrow and Wembley 1946—1947.
Spotted Flycatcher—A ; – ; C, 2 ; D. Breeds regularly Mount Park.
Pied Flycatcher—A ; Bred in nesting box on island on Dobbs Hill Pond 1904. Nest watched by T.L.B. and H. Park.
Goldcrest—A ; – ; – ; D. Local South Hill Avenue, Bury House and Ruislip.
Firecrest—D. 1943. Ruislip.
Chiffchaff—A ; B, 6 ; C, 8 ; D.
Willow Warbler—A ; B, 11 ; C, 12 ; D.
Wood Warbler— – ; B, 1 ; *C*, 2 ; –. Local to Copse Wood.
Grasshopper Warbler—A ; – ; C, 3 ; *D*. Favourite nesting place at Ruislip ploughed up 1942.
Reed Warbler— – ; B ; *D*. Bred Newton S.F. till 1928. Ruislip till 1945.
Sedge Warbler—A ; B, 3 ; C, 8 ; *D*.
Garden Warbler—A ; – ; C ; D.
Black Cap—A ; B, 3 ; C, 2 ; –.
Whitethroat—A ; B, 7 ; C, 9 ; D.
Lesser Whitethroat—A ; B, 4 ; C, 4 ; —.
Fieldfare—A ; B. 13 ; – ; D. Formerly abundant Roxbourne area.
Mistle-Thrush—A ; B, 10 ; C, 5 ; D.
Song Thrush—A ; B, 37 ; C. 12 ; D.
Redwing—A ; B, 14 ; C, 1 ; D. Large numbers Northolt, Eastcote, Ruislip 1941.
Ring-ouzel—A ; Newton Sewer Farm 1905.
Blackbird—A ; B, 36 ; C, 15 ; D.
Wheatear—A ; B, 2 ; C, 3 ; *D*.. Often seen in the very big field opposite Isolation Hospital up to 1914. Also Northwood Golf Course and more recently at Northolt Aerdrome.

Greenland Wheatear— – ; – ; C ; *D.* Local in May to field up Windmill Hill.
Whinchat—A ; B, 5 ; C, 3 ; –. Well distributed before 1930. Then local at Newton S.F., and Dump near " Clay Pigeon."
Stonechat—A ; B, 4 ; C, 5 ; *D.* Bred in built up area 91 Woodend Avenue and 45 Eastcote Lane up till 1940. Only the cock birds wintered in the district.
Redstart—A ; – ; – ; *D.* Never common. Seen Ruislip Common 1947.
Nightingale—A ; B ; C, 4 ; *D.* Sung in Roxeth up to 1938.
Robin—A : B. 39 ; C, 12 ; D.
Hedge Sparrow—A ; B, 26 ; C, 11 ; D.
Wren—A ; B, 27 ; C, 2 ; D.
Swallow—A ; B, 19 ; C, 5 ; D.
House Martin—A ; B, 18 ; C, 10 ; D.
Sand Martin—A ; B, 1 ; C, 5 ; *D.* Ceased nesting at Northwood Golf Links in 1910.
Swift—A ; B, 11 ; C, 8 ; D. Average arrival date at Gasometer 5th May.
Nightjar—A ; – ; *C* ; *D.*
Kingfisher—A ; B, 4 ; – ; D.
Green Woodpecker—A ; B, 4 ; C ; D.
Great Spotted Woodpecker—A ; – ; C ; D. Mount Park.
Lesser Spotted Woodpecker—A. Local at Eastcote.
Wryneck—A ; – ; – ; –. Bred in Temple's Orchard. Brought its young into Mr. O'Brien's orchid house 1915. Last seen Grove Farm Lane. Recorded by Mr. Tomkims, Brook Avenue 1929.
Cuckoo—A ; B, 7 ; C, 9 ; D.
Little Owl— – ; – ; C ; D.
Tawny Owl—A ; B, 4 ; – ; D.
Barn Owl—A ; B ; – ; –.
Kestrel—A ; B, 7 ; C, 4 ; D. Bred Harrow Steeple, 1946.
Sparrow Hawk—A ; B, 9 ; *C*, 1 ; *D.*
Heron—A ; B, 7 ; *C*, 1 ; *D.*
Bewick Swan—D. Ruislip 1939 and 1945.
Mute Swan— – ; B, 1 ; C, 9 ; D.
Barnacle Geese— – ; B 1 ; – ; –. With Brents 9/11/24. Ruislip Reservoir.
Brent Geese— – ; *B*, 2 ; – ; –. From 9/11/24 till 25/1/25 Ruislip Reservoir.
Ruddy Shelduck—*C*, 2. Ruislip 28/5/42.
Mallard—A ; B, 18 ; C, 11 ; D.
Teal— – ; B ; C, 7 ; *D.* Newton S.F. Winter visitor nested Ruislip 1941.
Pintail— – ; – ; *C*, 7 ; –.
Pochard— – ; *B*, 13 ; *C*, 1 ; *D.*
Tufted Duck— – ; *B*, 15 ; *C* ; *D* ;

Scaup—*C.* 30/3/41—5/4/41.
Wigeon— – ; *B*, 1 ; – ; –.
Pintail— – ; – ; *C*, 7 ; –.
Shoveler—A. Ruislip 1924.
Great Crested Grebe—A ; B, 21 ; C, 12 ; D. Stopped breeding at Ruislip 1943.
Little Grebe—A ; B, 17 ; – ; –.
Wood Pigeon—A ; B, 22 ; C, 12 ; D.
Stock Dove—A ; B, 3 ; C,; –.
Turtle Dove—A ; B ; C ; –.
Golden Plover—A ; B, 2 ; – ; D.
Lapwing—A ; B, 29 ; – ; D.
Common Sandpiper— – ; – ; C ; D.
Redshank—A ; – ; C ; –. Last seen Newton S.F. 1929.
Snipe—A ; B, 5 ; C, 3 ; *D*. Common at Newton S.F. till 1922. Still visits fields near " Clay Pigeon."
Jack Snipe— – ; B ; – ; D. Newton S.F. 1941 Ruislip 1943.
Woodcock— – ; B ; C ; –.
Common Tern. 10th October 1941.
Blackheaded Gull— – ; B, 4 ; C, 4 ; D.
Common Gull— – ; – ; C, 3 ; D.
Herring Gull— – ; B, 1 ; C, 1 ; D.
Lesser Black Back – ; – ; C ; D.
Arctic Skua—Roxeth 21st May 1943.
Corn Crake—A. Formerly common at Newton S.F. Not seen since 1924. Heard near Orley Farm 1940.
Water Rail—A. Visited water logged fields both sides of Long Mile.
Moorhen—A ; B, 25 ; C, 12 ; D.
Coot—A ; B, 34 ; C, 13 ; D.
Pheasant—A ; B, 16 ; C, 5 ; D.
Partridge—A ; B, 14 ; C, 4 ; –. Wanders along railways bank including Piccadilly near South Harrow Station.
Red Legged Partridge— – ; – ; *C. D.* Local to Mad Bess Wood area.

(*Copyright Photo by* VICTORIA AND ALBERT MUSEUM)

SALISBURY SPIRE—THE WORK OF ELIAS DE DERHAM, RECTOR OF HARROW
(INSET HARROW STEEPLE)

(*From original by* Max Hofler)

Looking Up To Harrow Steeple, 1923

(*From Drawing by* C. Stanfield, A.R.A.)

Looking Down on Roxeth Common, 1834

CHAPTER NINE

AROUND THE STEEPLE

(Rooks and Recorders).

IN " Place Names of Middlesex " G. E. B. Gover interpretes " HROCES-SEATH " as the pit, well, or lake of a man named HROC. " HROC " has been certified a pre-conquest personal name so that there is ground for supposing that a person named HROC may have left the imprint of his name on a " SEATH," an " EYE " a " BORW " and a " BURN " in our district and that Roxborough, Roxey, Roxeth and Roxbourne mark the bounds of his ancient domain. If so Barrow, Barrow Hill, and Roxs-Barrow may mark the place of internment of a giant of antiquity as great as Gog or Magog.

Having, however lived in the district for half a century and having counted a dozen rookeries along the Roxbourne, past Roxeth, and the Roxey marshes to the Priors Field, and having watched the nightly return of thousands of rooks to their ancestral Roxeth rookeries I can think of no more appropriate name for this ancient abode of birds than the ' Rooks marshland.'

The bird rooks, as well as the human folk named Rooks can claim a pre-norman pedigree. and it is likely that members of the rook bird family entered the county long before the Norman conqueror ordered his men to march up from Battersea, through Hayes and Roxeth, to cover his flank while he continued his slaughter and burnings in Buckinghamshire ; another branch of the rook family may have practised gliding across the Roxey marshes a million years before Wilbur Wright crashed into them.

Like the hamlet to which they gave their name our rooks have been much persecuted. Yet in spite of annual thinnings and shootings, and periodic scientific enquiries into their feeding habits, they have survived. Being sensible creatures, they like a mixed diet but as the proportion of wire worms to corn varies with each rook in each month in each county, dead rooks provide pestologists with much interesting data, from which to draw divergent conclusions, about the goodness or the badness of Rooks. Although the rook is partial to corn, perhaps he is not as black as he is painted ; and when you get as close to a living rook in the sunshine as Mrs. Brightwen did to Merops the tame rook in her Stanmore Garden, you may discover that " its plumage is a rich violet shading into dark blue near the head."

Rooks are interesting birds to watch at their parliaments, at their nests, and in the air ; and now that they are being replaced by gulls and aeroplanes in the skies above Harrow, it is interesting to speculate how long they have resided in the district. When, just after the ice age, the countryside was sparsely dotted with pines and birchwoods, siskins, crossbills and hardy hooded crows may have been more common than rooks. No doubt rooks increased as the cold birch forests gave way to warmer oak woodlands ; and when these were cut down rooks continued to thrive in the Roxeth cornfields.

Norden, who mapped and wrote about the country round Harrow noted that the oaks that had formerly been very famous for feeding the farmers' venison, had fallen to the ground " and it is scarcely known where they stood." Roxeth Grove has disappeared, but Harrow Grove has survived. Looking out from the terrace in 1585 Norden noted a vayne of the best wheatland in England ; but he lamented many things : —

1. The disappearance of good oak trees " It is a pitie the Lords of the Manor have not more care for their posterities."

2. The increase of old fruit trees and the decay of the art of making good cider and good perry " because the housewives are uttering the fruit in the market as they do other vendibles."

3. Most of all, like Thomas More in Utopia, he lamented the change over of much land from arable to pasture.

With all these changes there must have been alterations in Roxeth's bird life. The wryneck likes old fruit trees, and rooks and other birds take kindly to corn. Wrynecks nested regularly in Temple's old orchard and survived at Brook Avenue, Roxeth, until 1929. Farmlands always attract a rich, mixed population of birds ; along the Roxbourne, interspersed with the Rector's hay crops and corn shucks, there were marshes full of waterfowl, bittern, heron, and spoonbills. In a letter dated 1537 Richard Layton, the Harrow rector who despoiled Becket's shrine, wrote to his master Thomas Cromwell from his comfortable well feathered parsonage in the Hanging Gardens where the Speech Room now stands, " I send by this bringer pears of Harrowe graffed by my Lord Duresme, his own hands, and partriges my own hawk kills."

Two centuries later, when Daniel Lysons looked down on Roxeth Common from the terrace below the church, he assessed that the district was equal parts pasture and arable. The nightly movement of the rooks across Harrow skies, past the ruined church that sheltered the local fire engine in its tower, was then in full swing. At that time there was no Gilbert White to record the changing bird population of the rectory garden ; but for nearly 150 years since Lysons made his survey of Roxeth manor there has been an almost unbroken succession of rook counters and bird recorders at Harrow, and it may well be that the five mile circle round Harrow steeple has been better and more faithfully watched than any area of corresponding size in the whole of Britain.

WALTER TREVELYAN'S nature diary dates from 1812—1815. Twelve days after Waterloo the Harrow birds began to sing at half past two in the morning.

Whilst that eminent ornithologist DR. EDWARD HAMILTON, F.L.S., was at Harrow between 1828—1832, he occassionally saw Ravens ; and he records that MR. GOSHAWK the local bird stuffer, tried to get a pair that nested in Lord Northwicks grounds. After leaving Harrow Dr. Hamilton kept records of Hyde Park birds, and watched the Kensington Gardens rookery decline from 100 to 36 nests.

The next Harrow recorder was REV. H. J. TORRE (1831—1839). In his list of " Birds found in Middlesex, 1838," he left notes about crossbills, cornbuntings, woodlarks, curlews and a bittern that was shot at Harrow. His Diary for 7th May, 1838 states " About 100 nightingales were taken by Harrow bird catchers during the last week or ten days." NED POWELL was Harrow's most famous bird catcher. He knocked down a male crossbill with a stone near Harrow, and kept it in a cage. It was an old bird having the under parts spotted light red, and the back beautifully marked with green and red. It was said to have been with its brood of five when it was captured. One of the favourite snaring grounds was the lane between Roxeth and Pinner. Here some of the London bird catchers, with their nets and decoy birds slept on the job under arched canopies tunnelled into the tangled hedges which bordered both sides of the lane.

LORD LILFORD who became president of the British Ornithological Union was at Harrow from 1846—1850. J. H. SWAINSON from 1854—1860. The brothers F. G. and G. M. BRIDGEMAN were at Harrow from 1857—1864. They compiled a Harrow Bird List for Melvilles " Flora of Harrow " 1864. This included notes on the Rook and 92 other species. The improved drainage system which followed the famous 1850 enquiry into the health of the hamlets of Roxeth and Harrow caused the common snipe, jack snipe, and woodcock to leave the vicinity of the Hill ; but they went on increasing at Newton Sewer Farm well on into the 20th century. My first noteworthy record from this ' Farm ' was a Ring-Ouzel in the spring of 1905 and my last a Jack Snipe on 20th December, 1939.

Three bird recorders who spent much more than their school days at Harrow were C. A. CATER, who lived at Coran, Mount Park, M. E. GRAHAM and R. BOSWORTH SMITH. The last named was a master at the school from 1864 till 1901. He wrote " Bird Life and Lore," and states that during 17 of the years he was at Harrow, one of his most delightful pets and companions was Jacob, a tame Raven. About his time MRS. BRIGHTWEN, the aunt of Edmund Gosse, and the friend of Hooker, and the author of " Wild Nature won by kindness," was living at her beautiful residence The Grove, Stanmore, and enjoying the companionship of Zoe the Nuthatch and Merops the Rook.

In 1866 J. E. HARTING published his famous "Birds of Middlesex". This was the first of the County Ornithologies, but it would have been a rather slender volume if the Harrow and the Kingsbury Reservoir records had been omitted. He estimated that there were 1,320 rooks nesting in a Middlesex area five miles long and three miles broad. The annual white invasion of Harrow skies by four species of gulls had not yet begun, but Harting proudly recorded that he had seen (and confirmed by shooting) several Black headed Gulls at Kingsbury, a distance of 30 miles from the sea.

Hartings' "Birds of Middlesex" was brought up to date by W. E. GLEGG in 1935, but neither of these excellent books does justice to the bird life of the district between Roxeth and Ruislip. The reason being that this area was 'out of bounds' to many generations of Harrow School boy naturalists.

G. E. H. BARRETT HAMILTON brought the local bird list up to date in 1891. He recorded the rook as "resident and very numerous" and enumerated 196 other species including the last Harrow district records of the Dartford Warbler, Dipper, Pine Grossbreak, Hen Harrier, and Purple Heron. In this book also there are no references to Newton Sewer Farm and few to Ruislip Reservoir.

WINSTON CHURCHILL was at Harrow School from 1888—1892. Like King John and Chicken Andrews he kept dogs at Harrow ; but there is no record that he hunted rats round Roxeth Barn or looked for birds nests along the pleasant foot path that then led from Jolly's Alley to the Shooting Butts fields. We know that he gathered leaves for his silkworms from the old mulbery tree in Roxeth House and a picture of him sitting on the tall gate of this haunted house at the bottom of West Street has survived. There is also an interesting story that he scorched his face and singed his eyebrows exploding a bomb in the disused well of this great derelict 31 room house. Roxeth House was pulled down in 1892. Its grounds and Farmer Pring's fields were then levelled for use as an additional Harrow School cricket ground. The old Roxeth lower road was renamed Peterborough, and a stand was erected near the Horse Pond from which matches in both fields could be watched.

M. P. PRICE, was at Harrow from 1899 to 1903. Instead of summarising ancient rarity records he gave an interesting account of the rural scenery and the vertebrate fauna of the Harrow District. He listed 3 species of bats, 4 Insectvora, 11 Rodentia, 3 Carnivora, 63 Aves (Birds), 4 Reptiles and 4 Amphibians, making a modest total of 99. He realised that, though the numerous pretty green lanes round Roxeth were becoming haunts of navvies working on the new District and Great Central Railway, they were good haunts for birds—'chiefly all sorts of warblers.' I thoroughly agree with his verdict that "of these lanes the one leading from the Sewage Farm near Roxeth past the Rifle Range and ending eventually at Pinner was the best and the longest." His repeated references to this lane as the lane to Pinner help to confirm my suspicions that the lane was named after the Edwardian owner of Dabbs Hill, and not after a Victorian shepherd. It was certainly from this lane that Park's aviary which backed on to St. Hilda's stables (now 296 Northolt Road) was replenished with redpolls, mealy redpolls, siskins, goldfinches, twites, bullfinches, chaffinches, linnets, blackcaps and nightingales. I can confirm that the top school boys and the Roxeth chaws were largely and jointly responsible for the disappearance of nightingales from this lane.

Tizzies (Harrow school slang for sixpences) were harder to come by than eggs in Roxeth, and bantam eggs burned and painted to look like Kestrels eggs fetched a high price, especially if they were planted in old carrion crow nests. Butcher birds eggs and " Blood butcher birds eggs " (..the erythristic eggs of the red-backed shrike) taken in Roxeth, were also sure of a market on the hill. It is surprising how regularly these birds returned to the hedge which still borders the Eastcote Lane Cemetery. Like the Ruislip red-backed shrikes, these birds were clever at concealing their nests, and though many were robbed, some survived.

T. H. and W. R. D. HARRISSON were at Harrow from 1925—1930. They listed 157 bird species for the five miles round the steeple which was two more than W. E. Glegg had assembled for a much larger area, and twenty nine more than I was able to record for the much smaller area between Roxeth and Ruislip. T. H. Harrisson recorded 84 rooks nests within a four mile radius of Harrow in 1928. In 1929 there were 55 nests in the same area ; but in 1930 he counted 361 in the five mile radius . Since then counts have been made fairly regularly, but not always so thoroughly, and a steady decrease in rooks has been recorded both in the five mile Harrow circle and over the whole county. At the London Natural History Society census made in the spring of 1945, only 23 rookeries and 473 nests were enumerated in the whole of Middlesex. In a previous chapter I have explained how the rooks are leaving and the gulls are invading suburban areas. The last Roxeth rookery—the one situated at the back of St. Paul's Church, Corbins Lane, was abandoned in February 1945. I noticed, however, on 11th November, 1945, as Councillor F. A. Coles was beating the new Roxeth Boundary Stone at the bottom of the Long Mile, that a small new rookery had appeared just outside the Roxeth boundary. In 1946 no rooks bred in Roxeth, but in 1947 two nests in what was formerly Dabbs Hill Lodge Garden were occupied, and I saw young birds at the end of April. So the rook is breeding again in the Hroces-Seath area.

Roxeth bowlers carry a rook on their blazers and may be the Roxeth rook will one day lay down with the lion in the abundant foliage of the rather complicated Harrow Urban District Council coat of arms.

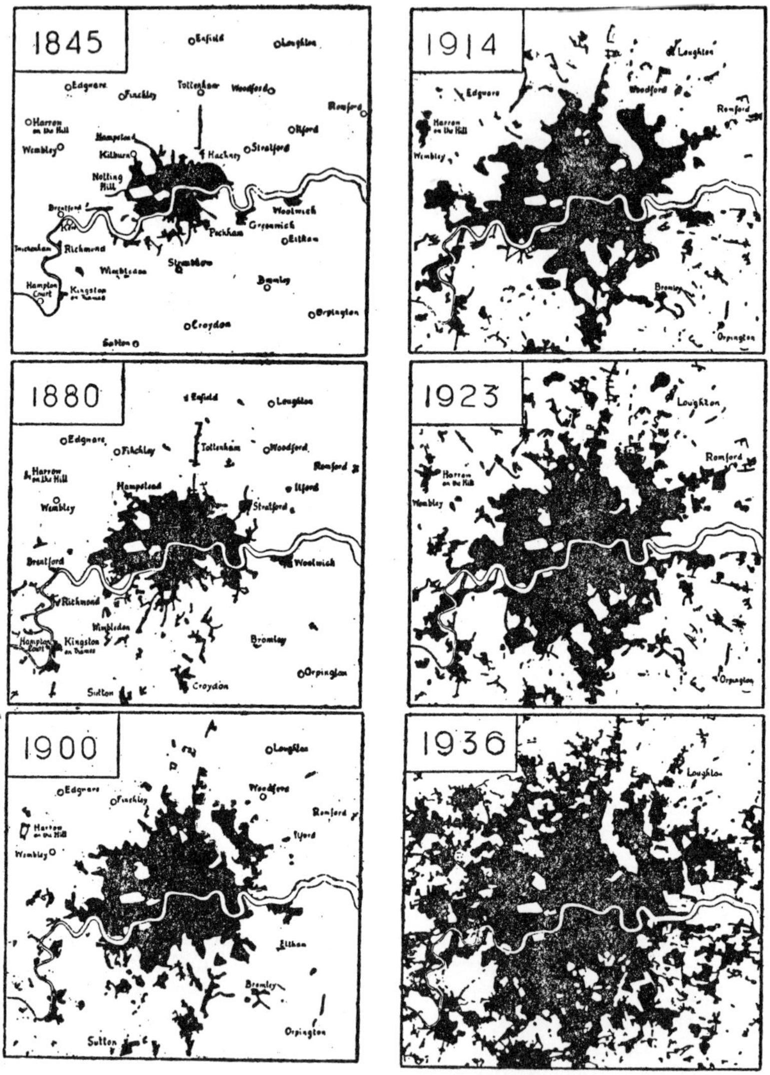

THE GREAT WEN showing the blacking out of Roxeth and Greater Harrow into Greater London.
(Reproduced by courtesy of the "Economist" and Messrs. George Allen and Unwin.

(*Photo by* Mitcham)
Northolt Footpath in 1912, Before the Racecourse Grand Stand was Erected

(*Photo by* Mitcham)
Northolt (Dobbs Mill) Lane. Now Main Approach to the Racecourse

PART III. THE CHALLENGE OF ROXETH

" *Thus saith the Lord : I am against the shepherds. I will make the places round My hill a blessing.*" *Ezekiel* 36.

CHAPTER TEN

ROXETH IN THE NINETIES

WHEN I came from Northolt to live in Roxeth between Barnett's Farm and Naylor's Nursery some fifty years ago, it was a pleasant rural hamlet. Its tithes had been commuted, and long strip cultivation of Roxeth's mediæval common fields had ceased. Roxeth had changed from a hamlet clustered round a green and blessed with an enormous common, to a big ecclesiastical parish. It was still a peaceful agricultural community made up of fields, and lanes, hayricks, barns and farm, but it had acquired a small Gas works, a Laundry, an isolation Hospital and rubbish and sewage depository. The face of Roxeth was still green, and though a main road (the central path through the old village green), held it together, it was most pleasantly intersected with ancient trackways, back lanes and footpaths. Three established routes ran southward across the parish—Woodend Lane, Cut Lane and Northolt Road. A fourth, the Roman straight Long Mile, separated Dobbs Tithing and Dabbs Hill Lodge, the home of the Greatorexes, from Newton tything, and Tithe Farm, the abode of Farmer Priest. A fifth, Pinner Lane (it was not called Rayners till 1916), led north westward in right angle bends towards Pinner. Then on the right of Northolt Road there were a number of short back lanes which took shape as farmers Wilson, Hollis and Jones hedged off their shares of old Roxeth Green. These Back Lanes were used for transferring sheep from field to field, or for bringing the cows in ; and they took the name of the farmer who used them most. Thus Grove Farm lane was successively known as Hawkins Lane and Fenwicks Lane. It is now called Park Lane. The lane now called Corbins was sometimes called Barnetts and sometimes Billy Goodchilds. Counting Grove Farm and Barnetts as six and seven, and Eastcote Lane as eight, Roxeth's ninth lane was called Eastcroft Lane or Halls Lane. It is now submerged in the gasworks, but formerly ran almost in a semicircle round what was apparently the old stockaded hamlet linking up with what is now known as Eastcote Lane, near Temple's Orchard. The numerous and rather dangerous bends at the Roxeth end of Eastcote Lane mark the dry route round the edge of the old ROXEYE marshes.

These green lanes and the footpaths that interlocked them were perhaps the most beautiful feature of old Roxeth. Woodend Lane led down hill from the Convent past the Nightingales Copse and the Gipsy Crowning Stone to Woodend Green. Much of Cut Lane—a very ancient trackway—had degenerated by the nineties into a footpath. It ran from Mount Park past Broomhill, down the present south arm of Brook Avenue, along the top of the present recreation ground and the back of Parkers Farm, to join and cross the main track from Roxeth Green (now called Northolt Road) at Northolt Stone or Stroud Gate. It then proceeded up Dabbs Mill or the Northolt Footpath Lane. This lane seemed to change abruptly into a footpath. Actually the old trackway turned sharply eastward at this point, and its very deep groove could be traced across the fields to Bourne farm and Uxbridge. This footpath route to Northolt Church, sometimes over a carpet of golden Elm leaves and sometimes through long grass, made a very pleasant Sunday Walk. Grove Farm, now called Park Lane, led right out into the fields. The name Roxeth Grove dates back at least to 1448 and possibly to 1282. It is shown on the old maps near where three Back lanes met, and close to the present junction of Park Lane and Park Mead. Everyone who remembers this trysting place agrees that it was one of the most beautiful corners of old Roxeth. Corbins Lane had a beautiful avenue of elms which made a complete arch over Barnett's cows as they trooped along it daily to be milked. This lane was rather spoiled by old Billy's pig sties, and the noticeable bulge in the middle of it was made long ago by folk who kept well on the right side of the lane so as to avoid the smells and other unpleasantnesses exuded by the piggeries. In Halls Lane there were interesting ponds and farm buildings, and I can still picture the corpulent landlord of the " Three Horse Shoes " disputing in this lane from his pony trap with the owner of a Russian performing bear. The longest, the most interesting, and the most beautiful lane was the one which led between the Wheatear field and the Isolation hospital, the Ashheap and the rookeries, the Shooting Butts and the Kingfishers field towards Pinner. W. W. Druett suggests that it was an ancient Anglo-Saxon trackway. It had a number of interesting right angle bends which linked up old pathways between the sellions, and the alignment of these sellions seems to be at right angles to the Roman bounds of the North Pagus. Sometimes this lane was very muddy, but at all seasons of the year it was thronged with birds. I could tell the season of the year not only by the birds and the blossoms, but by the human occupants of this lane. First fieldfares, blackthorn and gypsies. Next warblers, dog roses and birdcatchers and then old man's beard, haymakers and corncrakes. The gypsies were not always dirty idle vagrants. They hung their washing on the bushes, and sometimes sat in rings shaping clothes pegs and strengthening them with metal bindings collected from the ashheap. They cut withies and made plaited rush horsewhips and white nosegays from the linings of rushes to give to the children of the folk who bought their pegs.

Roxeth in the early nineties was not a bad place for a child to grow up. I was taught scripture and history at home and unlike other children who went to school when they were five I was allowed to run wild till I was nearly seven. At that time Roxeth had a beautiful new parish church not fifty years old, a Wesleyan chapel near Jollys Alley, and a wooden Salvation Army Barracks. Other parochial amenities were a lecture hall on Roxeth Hill given by Charles Leaf. He was also the principal donor of the Cottage Hospital in the Lower Roxeth Road. Normally the Lecture Hall was used for vestries, prayer meetings, and penny readings ; but in bad winters, and there were many in the nineties, it functioned as a soup kitchen. Most evenings I used to ride out of the hamlet at the back of a pony trap which splashed through the pond at the bottom of West Street on its way to pick up Mr. Hawkins, one of those distinguished folk who travelled every day to London. The idea of any one going daily to town from Roxeth was still quite a novelty.

Morning and afternoon on Sundays I went with my brothers and sisters to Sunday School. The Parish Hall (or Sunday School) was not yet built so we went to the Mission Hall (the present sub fire station) in Northolt Road. Mrs. Bayliss had an overflow department for infants at The Grange, and there was another overflow at a disused butchers shop where Mr. Barrington later let out bicycles.

The four public houses—The Timber Carriage—The Half Moon—The White Horse and The Three Horse Shoes seemed to loom larger then than they do today. They were much in demand at the thirsty haymaking time, when the hamlet was raided by an additional population. A number of these were regulars, and had definite corners in the great Roxeth barns ; but many were quite content to sleep in the hedges up Pinner Lane. When I was not at school I spent a good deal of my time in the barns, the ponds, the orchards, the glasshouses, the shrubberies, the stables and the fields which made up St. Hildas or Naylors Nursery as it was more commonly called.

Memories of those far off golden days at St. Hildas when I swung on the white gate, played smugglers in the barn, cruised round the lily pond and fed a great pike in a tank under a canopy of Mr. O'Brien's orchids, make me conscious of some of the shortcomings of our present day Recreation Grounds. Thanks to the persistence of Mr. John Short—" the member for Roxeth," just before the Diamond Jubilee Roxeth acquired two fields for recreation. These fields were up the Toll Gate Road. They were bordered by deep ditches and tall hawthorn hedges. They were full of buttercups skylarks' nests, ragged robins and shivery shakes. In the far corner there was a real pond, and in the untrimmed boundary oaks were natural cradles, where babies could be parked while their guardians paddled, fished for newts, or got right into the pond. These fields have evolved into the present Roxeth Recreation Ground ; and on Saturdays its rationed greensward is entirely allotted to adults for cricket or football, tennis, allotments or bowls.

Today the site of St. Hilda's (270—272 Northolt Road) is well used by the new Baptist Church. In the nineties it was a warm comfortable seventeenth century house. Its polished dancing floor and great oak beams shone in the firelight, and its six stairways seemed to be specially constructed for playing hide and seek. Many years later when Mr. Len Naylor and his family had gone to Australia, Toc H persuaded the Churches to use St. Hilda's fine old panelled room fitted with its great comfortable fireplace and corner cupboard as an " Open House " for young folk on Sunday evenings.

" To an open house in the evening
home shall all men come "

Ulysses built his house round a rooted oak converted into a bedstead : the seventeenth century folk built theirs round comfortable fireplaces; but then of course they had no hot water taps, (only warming pans) and none of our modern amenities. Their rations also were different. They thought in sides not in rashers of bacon.

There were seven farms—Barnetts, Hall's (Eastcrofts), Parker's, Priest's (Tithe Farm), Hawkin's (Grove Farm), Woodbridges and Honeybuns. There was a School Laundry up Alma Road but few other houses and old Alfred hung his washing out in his front garden opposite the very New Parish (1898) Hall. Roxeth's small Gasometer was not a scar on the sky line or a blot on the landscape. To us boys it seemed hardly larger and not so important as the Big Shed on the waste ground between the New Roads (Stanley and Sherwood) in which Mr. Fleet kept his balloon.

Except for the cottages near Valentine Road the only houses in Northolt Road beyond Mr. Jim Atkins on the right, and the empty saddler's shop now numbered 175, on the left, were three farm houses, three farm cottages and St. Hilda's.

Roxeth had one big shop, Sladdens, at Roxey corner and twenty-nine others along Middle and Northolt Roads. On the right Barnes, Enston, Polly Garrett, Simpkins, " The Three Horse Shoes," Dodds, Shorts, Liddiard, Underwood. On the left Higgs, Honeybun, Bentley, Goodchild, " The Half Moon," Sladdens, Wingroves, Ward, Cullens, " The Timber Carriage," Nobes, Leapers, Brown, Wheelers, Clarke, Shearlock, Davidge, Horns, Pratts, Abbots, and Frewing. Only two of these businesses have survived, Shearlocks the Grocers and Bentleys the Barbers.

(*Lent by* Misses Baggaley)

St. Hilda's (Naylors Nursery) Gardens 1884

(*Lent by* Mrs. Barnett)

Roxeth Farm (Barnetts) in 1888

Apart from shops and farms I doubt if there were then more than three hundred households in Roxeth, which would have given a population of about two thousand. In the nineties Roxeth was a place worth living in but perhaps even then its most vital and characteristic possessions were its worthies.

Has South Harrow anyone to compare with Old Alfred the lamplighter, with one legged Mr. John Short, the member for Roxeth, or with Sancho Payne the strong man who knocked the bell off the top of the strength tester at the Fair? Or with Sir William Perkins scrambling aniseed balls at Sunday School Treats and Lord Roberts of Kandahar passing through the district on his pushbike?

There were giants in those days. Six foot Farmer Priest who could clear a five bar gate like a stag, and seven foot Mr. Lascelles who ducked at every doorway as he passed round Gaffer Wright's School on a managerial visit, followed by Mr. Short the member for Roxeth.

While Sir William Perkins, the scientist, was blowing his trombone and enjoying himself at Sunday School treats, his factories at Greenford Green were becoming derelict and the aniline dye trade was passing to Germany. I attended his funeral in Roxeth Churchyard, and recollect the mountain of flowers and the tributes then paid to his genius by German science and German industry. I also remember the mounted horseguards who attended Dr. Stivens' funeral in the same churchyard.

Of honourable God-serving women there were not a few and with proud thanksgiving I remember my old Sunday School teachers, Mrs. Bayliss of " The Grange," Miss Perkins, daughter of Sir William, Miss Mabel Jones, daughter of the General and many others. The names of some of Roxeth's good women survive on mossy tombstones and on the many coloured windows of the little church they consecrated. The names of their sons appear in leaded and painted letters in the stone and wooden memorials which were well and truly fixed, by their comrades, to the walls of Roxeth Church and the Roxeth Men's Institute.

1914......1918

In honoured and loving memory of our brothers. Who leaving ROXETH to fight for King and Country. Fell in that just cause—Whose souls are in the hand of God.

W. C. Adams	H. J. Greenfield	H. Neil
J. H. Baggaley	C. W. A. Halliday	C. Norman
J. Barnett	A. C. Harman	A. J. Peavot
E. C. Baul	S. B. Hawes	B. C. Perrott
E. A. Bennion	W. G. Heales	A. G. Pratt
C. H. Bird	C. V. Hepworth	H. F. Ridgeway
J. C. Bodimeade	E. A. Herbert	W. G. Ryder
W. Boffin	C. E. Hickson	C. F. Roberts

C. Bradbury
A. W. Branch
A. Brayshaw
J. H. Brooks
H. A. Brown
S. G. Burnham
W. Burnham
W. H. Clowes
W. F. Cobb
A. J. Davidge
A. W. Day
H. Dean
C. Ellerington
F. Field
S. G. Garwood
J. Grant
C. W. Hilsden
W. T. Hirt
F. S. Hiscox
E. C. Holloway
A. Horne
C. E. Jelly
A. J. Jolley
W. T. Kirby
R. Leaper
E. Lee
H. Lee
H. G. Leek
H. A. G. Mallet
F. Maloney
S. C. Marshall
W. P. Masters
R. W. W. Meades
A. B. Moreby
T. H. Salisbury
W. F. Salisbury
A. F. Sharp
E. H. Sharp
M. H. I. Shepherd
H. S. Sherwood
E. Smith
E. G. Squibb
A. E. Stiles
R. H. Thomas
J. O. Tomlins
W. L. Troke
H. G. Turner
C. A. Werner
F. C. White
W. Wright

I thought my schoolmates would come marching
In the days that were to be
Down the long main road of Roxeth
To the sound of minstrelsy.
But those comrades now are sleeping
Far from England's circling wave:
And Olympian snows are keeping
Watch o'er many a Roxeth grave.
Vimy, Zion, and Olympus
Lift your foreheads to the sky
Tell the coming generations
That you heard them Marching by.

Sometimes as I wait for a bus at Roxeth Corner I try to reconstruct a picture of what it looked like fifty years ago. The Board School bell is ringing loud up the hill across the meadows. The sparks are flying from Mr. Nobes' forge, and Mr. Ward's clock (its square pane remains!) says it is two minutes to nine. I shall be late for having stopped to open the gate to the Grange for Mrs. Bayliss in her quaint little tub pony trap, and having received an enchantingly Victorian, smile of approval, I am now not looking forward to Gaffer Wright's strap. It hurt much more than the withies which bearded Gaffer Wilkinson allowed you to choose and cut for yourself. Unfortunately Bill Elliott who looked out on this scene for twenty years from his bath chair did not sketch. He just amused himself making and glueing cork edged picture frames, and so it comes about that although we have old photos of the Half Moon and Sladdens, no adequate Constable picture of the other side of the road has survived. A mixed hedge of hawthorn, rosebriars, and brambles ran from Roxeth Corner to the railings of the new Parish Hall. It was broken only by a lane leading to Mount Pleasant Cottages and by the long shady drive to the Grange. Behind this hedge was a second screen of elms, horsechestnuts and weeping willows, which half hid, half framed the cottages, the pond, the Grange and the Great Barn. Here, not on the shopping side of the road, the heart of old Roxeth lies bleeding. For some inexplicable reason this heart and core of old Roxeth has been labelled West Harrow Ward. It is one hundred per cent Roxeth. It lies south of the steeple and none of it is in the West Harrow Parliamentary Division.

I will conclude my memories of Roxeth in the nineties with a story of Alfred the Lamplighter. The farthest street lamp in the south of the parish was at the bottom of Valentine Road. We used that post as a sounding board for our game of " Kick-Can Kick " until it was dark enough to play " Dick, Dick Show Light " or " Tag Button." From this point old Alfred, carrying his light on the end of a long pole, set out on his nightly rounds. " Where be ee going Alfred? " " Up and over and round the Hill! " He was a queer cove but when my brother got lost after the Jubilee Bonfire in the Church fields, it was old Alfred who brought him back all the way from Wealdstone. In those days there were several witches living in the neighbourhood and a terrible person called " Spring Heel Jack " waylaid late travellers on the darksome lonely Northolt Road. It was said that this white apparition scared at least one person to death. " Jack the Ripper " was also in the news. So after poor old Alfred had been primed in the horrors by some of his pals at the Gas Works, they hid with a white sheet in Harrow Churchyard, and just as the clock struck twelve they jumped on their victim. No doubt Alfred was frightened, but his response was characteristic—" I don't care if you are a Ghost! I don't care if you are a Spirit! The Lord is on my side." So was the lamplighter's baton, and one of " the Ghosts " from the Gasworks had to be taken to the Cottage Hospital!

CHAPTER ELEVEN

CHURCH AND PARISH

THE ecclesiastical parish of Roxeth dates from 1863 ; so that, compared with Roxeth Manor or Roxeth hamlet it is comparatively modern. Being formed from the civil parishes of Wembley and Harrow on the Hill, it at first incorporated most of Roxeth hamlet and a good deal of the countryside round Greenford Road. Until St. Paul's Roxeth was taken from it, the little parish church on Roxeth Hill served everyone who lived west of " The Rising Sun " as far as the Pinner Lane Shooting Butts ; and South of John Lyon School as far as the Long Mile Boundary Stone. This area was about four times as large as the present parish of Christ Church, and more than three times as large as the present H.U.D.C. ward called Roxeth.

Roxeth Parish Church was built of flint and stones in 1862. Its name Christ Church links it with Abbot Werhard and the Christ Church monks of 830 A.D. It is pleasantly situated in a green valley on the slopes of Roxeth Hill, its cruciform outline being half hidden by a giant Douglas Fir. Its modest steeple carries a clock and eight well tuned bells. It has a comfortable, inviting interior, which is adorned by four large colourful windows. These windows are memorials to John Chapman, Dr. Lambert, the Hallidays, and Barbara Hickman. There are smaller memorials, brasses and plaques to Rev. W. J. Knott, 1870, the first Vicar, to Anna Dodgson 1877, Kathleen Mary Gladstone 1889, Old Parishoners 1892, Otto Penniger 1907, Mrs. Temple of Southlands 1911 and a small brass memorial to Margaret Ruth Gardner 1919, from the children of Roxeth. Miss Ruth was as good a friend to Roxeth girls as her brother Charles was to Roxeth boys. During the 1914—18 War every road in old Roxeth parish lost at least one man, and the names of 76 Roxeth men are graven in leaded letters on a memorial on the northern outside wall of the Church. On weathered stones in Roxeth churchyard the following honoured names of forefathers of the old hamlet are discernible. Rev. William Horne (Vicar 1866—73). Richard John Chapman 1816—1884 of The Grange Roxeth. As an authority on the drainage of the area he was a principal witness at the Public Health Enquiry of 1849. His ivy shrouded tomb is a connecting link between the old Manor and the new ecclesiastical parish. John Martin 1887 (Sexton). William Nobes 1890 (Farrier).

John Chapman 1894 (of the Gas Works—a church worker and parish benefactor). James Naylor 1901 (of St. Hilda's Nursery). Alfred Arthur Priest 1915 (of Tythe Farm). Sir William Henry Perkins 1838—1907 (the famous scientist who first produced exquisite dyes from coal tar. He owned land in Roxeth and willed that no public house should be erected at any future time on that land). James Barnett 1916 (of Roxeth Farm). Rev. W. Done Bushell 1838—1917 (the learned historian of Harrow Church and author of the Octo Centenary Tracts. He lived at The Hermitage, one of the oldest inhabited sites of the Harrow district. Bowden House is now inscribed on the entrance gate, but it was long known as Le Ermitage and St. Edmunds Hermitage). William Pratt 1918 (his horse carts carried coal from the Metropolitan siding to the Gas Works). James Hawkins 1920 (As chairman of the Council he welcomed King Edward VII to Harrow). Henry Sherwood 1923 (of "The Highlands," churchwarden). Joseph Macandrew 1928 (of Dudley lodge, for many years the Vicar's warden). J. N. Stuart (of Broomhill, for many years the Peoples warden of Roxeth and President of most of its clubs and societies—a generous benefactor to the Parish and the Hospital). Joseph and Sarah Bayliss 1929 (For nearly half a century they were sexton and verger of Roxeth Church). J. C. Shearlock 1934 (grocer). James Atkins 1938 (builder). John Smith 1942 (builder).

Good old Roxeth was blessed for many years with a long unbroken line of good Sunday school teachers. Morning Sunday School, afternoon Sunday School, plus a childrens' service at the Lecture Hall under the superintendence of Mr. John Chapman, Mr. Len Naylor or Mr Frank Weatherley, was the normal Sunday routine for most of the children of Roxeth parish until 1914. There was however such a rich individuality about the teachers that even without the stimulas of Prize Givings and frequent treats at "The Grange," "Tithe Farm" and "The Cocoa Tree Grounds" at Pinner, this routine way of spending Sunday was far from boring. There was something joyous about the meeting of the rival crocodiles from Roxeth and Greenford Road for the service at the Lecture Hall. It was opened by the Rev. J. F. Andrews saying as if he meant it, "Before I go to my services in the church I should like to hear you children sing the Jubilate Deo on page ten." Although he had such a big parish he seemed to know every grown-up and every child in it. He regarded everyone who dwelt in his parish as part of his flock whether they attended church or not and before he left Roxeth he achieved his ambition of giving his parish the finest Parish Hall in the district. His predecessors were Rev. J. W. Knott 1862, Rev. W. Horne 1866, Rev. S. C. Morgan 1873 and Rev. J. Barton 1877.

His successor 1907—1912 was the Rev. F. R. Peachey—a man's man who wore a robin red breast waistcoat. He encouraged men to run an orchestra in their own way inside the church and to run their Institute as it seemed good unto them. His name is graven in stone on the Men's Institute and he is remembered with honour in Roxeth.

He was succeeded by the Rev. A. H. W. Ridsdale, 1912—1936, who had a charming wife and a charming daughter, willing and able to give the " Guides " and the " Cubs " just the sort of help and friendly hospitality they needed. Unfortunately as the number of houses in Roxeth increased, the supply of Sunday School teachers dwindled, but Scouting and Guiding helped to bridge the gap and when the Rev. J. N. Hoare arrived in Roxeth, Old Boys of the 12th Harrow (Roxeth Church) Scouts were ringing the bells, singing in the choir, teaching and superintending in the Sunday School, running the Y.P.U., running the Roxeth Men's Institute, running the Scout Troop, serving on the church council, painting the church gates and generally making themselves useful to their old Parish Church.

During the Incumbency of the Rev. J. N. Hoare (1937—1945) a lot of young Roxeth people were away from their parish on war service. Some did not return. In their absence Churchwardens were appointed from outside the parish and many changes were legally and easily made. Some of these were deeply resented by old residents, by young men and by scouts ; for they were deprived of accommodation which they had enjoyed for sixty, thirty and twenty-one years respectively. On the credit side the Vicar got the use of a new Vicarage, and the Hospital, began to make full and good use of the old Vicarage as a Nurses' Hostel. This was much needed as the Roxeth Cottage Hospital had evolved into the Harrow and Wealdstone District Hospital. The Sexton (thanks to Mrs. Sherwood) got a new cottage and there was no diminution in the missionary collections. Roxeth Church has always taken a keen interest in foreign missions, and regards Doctor (now Sir) Henry Holland as its own missionary!

The marriage in 1947 of the Rev. G. H. Spinney, Vicar of Christ Church, to the assistant matron of the Hospital has helped to federate the mutual interest of the Church and the Hospital in the South side of Roxeth Hill. This area formerly known as " The Waste " " Roxeth Waste " or " The Lord's Waste " was a bone of contention between the Roxeth folk and the Harrow Lord of the Manor. It is now a quiet sanctuary and place of healing. Pictures not only of the Church and the Hospital, but of the Parish Hall and the Gas Works, appear on the cover of the new parish magazine. This linking up of the prayer and work of the Church and Parish is in accord with the best Christ Church Benedictine tradition " Laborare est orare."

The great unsightly Roxeth gasometer has its feet set deep in our ancient stockaded village. It casts its shadow across the cassate of land which Abbot Werhard bought back as a community centre for his Benedictine brothers. Yet the gasometer is in a practical way continuing their radiant work of illuminating the neighbourhood beyond its own ancient bounds.

(*Photo by* G. E. Brock)

Christ Church, Roxeth

(*Photo by* G. E. Brock)

Roxeth Hill National Schools, Opened 1839

Roxeth Institute, 1904

The traditions of Edmund Rich and Shaftesbury, Becket and Churchill are curiously interwoven in our national and local stories ; but time may yet prove that the sufferings and goodness of Hroces-Seath are as old and as enduring as the triumphs and the greatness of Herga. If it is more blessed to give than to receive, Roxeth must be thrice blessed for she helped to give Harrow Church its stipend and steeple ; Harrow School its Fourth Form Room and Cricket Ground ; and Harrow and Wealdstone their place of healing. Roxeth has been stripped of its Green, its Waste, and its Common. It has been despitefully used, exploited, and dismembered ; but its ancient name, its Roman straight boundaries and its tradition for goodness remain.

ROXETH BENEFACTIONS

In addition to a long line of good vicars, notable churchwardens, and faithful sunday school teachers, the old hamlet had a number of generous benefactors. The following italicised extracts are taken from the Harrow Directory for 1937.

1. *The Church Room adjoining the Vicarage was built in* 1869 *by C. J. Leaf, Esq., and will seat* 100. It has been taken over by the Harrow Hospital and is serving a useful purpose.

2. *The Sunday Schools and Parish Hall in Northolt Road were built in* 1898. *The Hall seating* 400 *persons.* There is a tendency for it to be used more for Church than Parish purposes.

3. *The Men's Institute in Northolt Road built in* 1909 *has reading and recreation rooms.* After serving the young men of the Parish well for nearly thirty years it was obliged to close down on 30th June, 1938. See " Harrow Observer " 1/7/38.

4. The Infants Hut was given by J. N. Stuart in 1922. The 12th Harrow (Roxeth Church) Scouts enjoyed a use of it between 22nd April, 1924 and 17th April, 1945.

5. *The Mission Room built in* 1881 *by John Chapman was formerly in connection with Christ Church but has been taken over by the Fire Brigade.*

6. The Cottage Hospital. In 1896, Walford wrote " There is also a Cottage Hospital in the Roxeth Road on land given by Mr. Charles Leaf who bore the principal expenses of the building erected in 1872." This building was destroyed by a bomb in 1945, but its very grown up child flourishes on Roxeth Hill as the Harrow and Wealdstone Hospital.

Four other Benefactions not relating exclusively to Roxeth are worth noting.

7. In 832 Abbot Werhard's bequest of 1200 loaves with cheese or bacon fat on the aniverssarium of Wulfred.

8. In 1590 John Lyon's bequest of a Free Grammar School for the Parish.

9. In 1611 Katherine Clerke's bequest of £240 was distributed in 10/- sums to poor folk in Harrow and Roxeth.

10. In 1780 Margaret Parr's £200 bequest provided bread for poor of Harrow. Roxeth, Sudbury and Greenhill.

TWO BRASSES IN HARROW CHURCH

Heare lyeth buryed the bodye of John Lyon late of Preston. In this PISH yeoman Deceased the III day of October in the yeare of our Lord, 1592 who hath founded a free Grammer Schoolc in this Pish to have continuance for ever and for maintenance thereof and for releyfe of the poore and of some poore schollers in the universityes repairinge of high wayes and other good and charitable uses hath made conveyance of lands of good value to a corporation granted for that purpose Prayse be to the author of al goodness who make us mindful to follow his good example.

Here lieth the body of Katherine Clerke, daughter of Thomas Martin, widow of R. Clerke of Rislipe buried at Heyes. . . . she gave in her lifetime towards the maintenance for ever of XII poore people VI dwelling in Harrow Hill and VI in ROCKSYE. She died in London 26.XII.1613 being 84 years of age. "Who was in season as full of ripened corn. Brought hether where and whence she was borne."

ROXETH CLUBS AND ASSOCIATIONS

Just when the 'bloodie and murdering practice of football' and 'the refined game of cricket' replaced archery, cudgelling, cock fighting and maypoles on the Commons, the Wastes and the Greens of Roxeth I do not know ; but Roxeth certainly had village cricket and football teams before I came to live in the parish, and these associations and the old Volunteers, who had a Drill Hall near the 'Three Horse Shoes' and fine Shooting Butts up Pinner Lane, helped to weld the old hamlet happily together. By the kindness of Mr. Samuel Gardner and his sons, old folk and young folk shared the field at the rear of Mr. Chapman's Mission Hall (the present sub fire station). The activities included cricket and games, drill and quoits, and both the Institute and the Church Lad's Brigade seem to have originated in this field. The Roxeth Churchwardens, who were usually men of substance and goodwill, normally acted as Presidents and patrons of the village clubs, and ladies from Mount Park organised 'Bands of Hope' 'Scripture Unions' 'Penny Readings,' 'Soup Kitchens' and other parochial services and amenities. Each road had its District Visitor, and in this respect some roads were very lucky.

THE ROXETH MEN'S INSTITUTE

When Roxeth 'Die Hards' 'Sharp Shooters' and C.I.V's returned from the Boer War the Roxeth Men's Institute took on a new lease of life. Ropes and rings were fitted to the roof of the Parish Hall and Athletic and Gymnastics, as well as, Cricket and Football Teams were formed. The invincible "Harrow Mouchers" were beaten on their own ground, and when the football match on Roxeth Recreation Ground was between the Brigade Old Boys and The Institute, local enthusiasm rose high ; almost as high as at the annual tug of war final at the Flower Show between " The Police " and " The Gas Works." By 1909 the Institute had a home of its own, and it could then meet every night instead of hiring the Parish Hall for three nights. Activities ranged from Shovehalfpenny and quoits to chess and Marathon training. There was a well used Library. The Men's Service Orchestra gave spirit to services in the Parish Church, and tone to dances in the Parish Hall : and what about those Men's Suppers? In their heartiness they resembled the old " Church Ales," and they were in keeping with the spirit of the old hamlet : "Dost thou think because thou art virtuous there shall be no more cakes and ale?" The Institute continued to serve the parish by organising much needed healthy outdoor exercise right up to 1938, when it was closed down most unfortunately, but quite legally, by the Rev. J. N. Hoare, LL.B.

BRITISH LEGION CLUB

A unit of the British Legion began to operate in Roxeth in 1918, and after enjoying accommodation at "The Three Horse Shoes" " Wesley Hall " and a " Hut " behind Simpkins at Roxeth Corner, the present fine premises in Northolt Road were acquired in 1928. Its benevolent activities cover the whole of the H.U.D.C. area, and having a well equipped Hall, a Rifle Range and a Bar, it caters for a wide variety of tastes and interests. Its popularity is evidenced by a membership roll totalling eleven hundred. The President is Rev. G. H. Wooley V.C., Vicar of Harrow. The Chairman is Mr. F. H. Goodhead, who also helps to run the Library Service at Welldon Park School and the Roxeth Allotment Association. The Secretary of the British Legion is Mr. A. E. Sampson, 37 Kingsley Road, Roxeth.

TOC H

Although a handful of Toc H members were working in the district from 1919, the first regular meeting was not held till 26th October, 1926. It took place in the Leaf Memorial (Lecture) Hall, Roxeth Hill. The unit then sampled seven other meeting places before settling down to the rooms at 6 Crown Street. On 9th December, 1933, the Harrow Lamp, which is dedicated to Charles Gardner and the Elder Brethren of Harrow, was lit by the Prince of Wales in the Albert Hall. " One candle lights many," and Harrow soon became the parent Branch of many other Toc H units. Toc H aims at working *with* folk as well as *for* them, and by co-operating with individuals and associations who were interested in Christianity in Youth, in unemployed men, in hospitals, blind folk, prisoners, lepers and other good causes, Toc H has in a quiet way been of some service to individuals and to the local community. Its aims are set out in the Toc H Main Resolution.

Its meetings, held at 8 p.m. each Thursday night at 6 Crown Street, are open to Everyman. Its Honorary Secretary is Cyril

Ford, 36 Halsbury Road East, Northolt Park. The womens section of Toc H meets on Monday evenings at 6 Crown Street. Their Lamp, dedicated to Mary Jane Lovell 1849—1932, Mother of the Blind in Palestine was first lit by the present Queen (then Duchess of York).

CHURCH LADS' BRIGADE

No account of Roxeth since the Jubilee would be complete without a generous reference to the Roxeth and Harrow Company of the Church Lads' Brigade. They were first in the field so far as Roxeth boys' organisations were concerned, and fortunately they have been able to remain in possession of their splendid field in Northolt Road. This is well equipped with a chapel and with a Memorial Hall to Charles Gardner (1880—1920) their beloved Captain and benefactor, who lost his own life at the summer camp of 1920 trying to save two of the cadets from drowning. It would be difficult to list all the competition successes of the Roxeth Brigade Boys but it is not too much to state that in upholding the good name of Roxeth, they set the standard and the pace to all C.L.B. companies in the London diocese. My first memory of the Brigade was in 1898, when I marched behind their band on my way home from a Sunday School Treat at Bricket Woods. There were no buses in those days between Wealdstone Station and Roxeth. The Rev. F. R. Peerless, Chaplain of the Roxeth and Harrow Company, is also the C.L.B. Secretary at C.L.B. National H.Q. 58 Gloucester Place, W.1.

ROXETH BOY SCOUTS ASSOCIATION

Until quite recently Roxeth could provide ideal facilities for outdoor scouting especially up Pinner (Rayners) Lane. Some of the first scouts to camp in the open air after Baden Powell's pioneer camp on Brownsea Island, camped in Farmer Priest's hay fields at Tythe Barn. I watched them settling in and remember the comments that were passed on their " shorts," which caused almost as great a stir as the " bloomers " worn by women cyclists.

The first troop to be formed in Roxeth was the SEVENTH Harrow. It has always been attached to Roxeth Baptist Church. It has a lively Cub Pack under Miss Hilda Wildman, a real product of good old Roxey. Its founder, " Uncle Arthur " (Mr. A. E. Tapling), is now Treasurer both of the Roxeth and of the Middlesex County Boy Scouts Associations.

The second troop to be formed in Roxeth was the TWELFTH Harrow (Roxeth Church) Troop. Their amber and black Troop scarf is tied with a characteristic four square knot. This and the troop motto " Quis Separabit " reminds past and present members that they have a four fold allegiance to their Parish, their Parish Church, the family of Toc H, and the world wide Brotherhood of Scouts. This troop has held all the Harrow Cub, Scout and Rover trophies, and has ranked as second troop in the County of

Middlesex. It has an Old Boys' Association of 200 members.

Eight old boys of the troop were called to Higher Service during the 1939—1945 War, and friends of the troop are planning to provide the troop with a " Home of its Own " as a memorial to " Harry Creed, Ron. Fuller, Desmond Fitzgerald, Doug. Hamilton, Bill Kent, Bert Newey, Alf Riches, Reg Stiles, George Simpson, Taffy Withell, Peter Woodham—the Elder Brethren of the 12th Harrow." Mr. A. E. Tapling, 12 Earls Crescent, Wealstone, is treasurer of the Fund.

The following troops were formed after or whilst the hamlet was changing into a suburb. They bring the registered strength of the Roxeth Boys Scouts Association up to 570 members : The 3rd (open), The 5th (Eastcote Lane School), The 6th (St. Pauls' Church), The 8th (Methodist), The 9th (St Andrews Church), The 10th (Christ Church). The address of the District Commissoner, Keith Wilson, is 12 Whitehall Road, Harrow.

1945 was a memorable year for Roxeth Scouting. In addition to V.E. Day, and the 12th Harrow Coming of Age, a new Roxeth (not South Harrow!) Scout Association came into being on 2nd June and on 11th November Roxeth Rovers beat the bounds of their Parish.

Scouting is something more than an indoor club. It aims at producing happy, healthy and useful citizens. For Scouting as B.P. planned it, fresh air and sufficient space to exercise and spread canvas is needed. Where can these be found in the packed dormitory which has replaced old Roxeth? If you have any suggestions let the Friends of Roxeth know!

CHAPTER TWELVE

THE CHALLENGE OF ROXETH

FOR eleven centuries the good earth which lies in the path of the setting sun to the south and to the west of Harrow Hill, from " The Roxborough " along " The Roxbourne " to the bottom of the Long Mile, rejoiced in the name of Roxeth.

It was rich, fertile earth which produced good food for man and beast. Amongst the owners or occupiers of its moated manor ground were six kings (Offa, William Rufus, Stephen, John, Richard II and Henry VIII), over fifty archbishops from Wulfred to Cranmer, several Constables of the Tower and such interesting characters as Stidbert the Holy Man, Pilheard the noble, Weremberht the Thane, Werhard the Abbot, Leofwine the brother of Harold, Hamo de Roxesie, William the Outlaw, Nicholas Brembre, the Norths and the Dudleys, the Pitts and the Percivals, the relatives of David Garrick, the Greenhills, Blunts and Chapmans, Victorian Mrs. Bayliss and the Halls who became the residuary legatees of two arch—episcopal moats.

Roxeth had good reason to be proud of its ancient good name (Hroces-Seath) ; its size (From Ascot Bush to Heggestone); its status (a manor, a hamlet, a parish); its rich crops (wheat and hay), and its abundant health-giving open spaces (Roxeth Green, Roxeth Waste, and Roxeth Common).

The incorporation of the fertile Roxeth Vale into Harrow on the Hill followed swift on the loss of its common land. Then when Roxeth ecclesiastical parish spread eastward in 1863 folk forgot that the rich agricultural land north of Roxeth Common (Harrow School Cricket Field) was once part of Roxeth, and that the farmers of Honeybun, and Roxborough were important members of the old Roxeth Community.

It is strange, now that Parkers Farm, St. Hildas, Eastcroft, Dudley Lodge, Roxeth House, Honeybun's Farm and Roxborough Farm have all been pulled down, that two farms both claiming the name Roxeth Farm should have survived. One of these farms, also known as " Barnetts," is opposite the Roxeth Odeon Cinema, the other, also known as " Woodbridges," adjoins the Harrow School Cricket Field. New arrivals in the district who want to know what old Roxeth was like should look at these two surviving Roxeth farm houses.

It is also interesting, now that Roxeth's three tythings are almost covered with suburban houses, to record that the moated core of the Old Manor has survived. Eastcroft, the old home of the Halls, has been obliterated by the Gasworks, but horses that pull carts full of bottled milk still crop the old Manor fields ; and unwanted pears drop into a moat that has seen three hundred thousand sunsets.

Thus two farms, an ancient moat, an enormous barn and two fields remain to link suburbia with the proud days that are past. Treasure has been found near the Roxeth Moat, and more treasure remains. Maybe the National authorities who scheduled the Moat will return and make a fuller survey, or perhaps the new Edgware and Harrow Historical Society may decide to visit and report on the Great Barn and the Homestead Moat at Roxeth Grange.

Now that old Roxeth has more rate-payers than Canterbury there are valid practical reasons why its residents should follow the precedents of Headstone and Ruislip, and plan for a wise preservation of what little remains of their ancient heritage.

Not everyone is interested in history, but everyone needs sunlight and fresh air, and no part of Greater Harrow is worse provided with open space for its growing children than the over built area which lies to the west of Roxeth Grange.

It stands to the credit of the Harrow Urban District Council that, except in the use of West Harrow as a ward name, they have not accepted railway misnamings of the Roxeth area. Roxeth still appears as the name of Roxeth Parish area on the H.U.D.C. maps. Two boundary stones marked Roxeth 845 A.D. were set up by the H.U.D.C. on their old sites in 1945, and since then a Roxeth Civic Restaurant has been opened in Northolt Road.

There are already five roads running under the District Railway Viaduct ; so there is no justification for using this railway to break up the ancient three-ward unity of Roxeth. There is a north and south Pinner with Headstone, a north and south Wealdstone with Harrow Weald, a north and south Stanmore with Queensbury. If there were also a north and south Roxeth with Roxbourne, the chance of Greater Harrow developing an understandable five fingered unity for its fifteen wards would be greatly increased, and the chance of it developing into a meaningless suburban hotch potch of railway divided, railway named wards would be lessened.

An excellent multi-coloured Town Planning Map of Greater Harrow has been prepared. On this the Roxeth Grange Site (adjoining that very purple patch the Roxeth Gas Works) is depicted pure white, and Friends of Roxeth from all denominations and of different political colours have petitioned the Council to have this white oblong round the Roxeth Moat on the Town Planning Map repainted dark green to indicate that it has been scheduled for permanent preservation.

BUILDING THE SPIRE

Spires and boundary stones, vision and grit have played a part in shaping the story of Harrow. The foundations of Harrow were laid long before hand chipped flints appeared in its soil and because its Hill had grit and was well grounded it survived many ice ages and many floods. Dragons with wings bigger than eagles flew round it. Cumbersome monsters feeding in the marshes looked up to it. Bright little creatures carrying flint axes and later metalled spears (GARA) climbed to the top of it, and when a heathen temple (HEARGE) on the crest of the hill had served its purpose, and been broken down, and when Lanfranc's (IN GARA LANFRANCEUSTENET HEARGE) own church was falling into decay, Rector Elias de Derham, the architect of Salisbury Cathedral appeared on the scene.

Rector: This is a fine site Vicar . . . and what a sunset.
Vicar: Yes, Master Elias.
Rector: We must tithe the wool, the cheese, the Milk, the chickens and the little pigs and find the wherewithal to rebuild this church.
Vicar: Yes, Master Elias, but our tithes will not yield enough.
Rector: Then we must tithe the hay.
Vicar: Can we?
Rector: I will see Edmund Rich the new Archbishop, but first let boundary stones be set round the hayfields that have been recovered from the marshes. Who farms those rich lands towards the sunset?
Vicar: Hamon and Hugh of Roxesie. They are staunch supporters of Holy Church.
Rector: Good! We will bless their fields and hold a harvest thanksgiving at the Eastcote Bush.

And so after more talk and more planning the practical visionary got his way. A spire appeared on the crest of Harrow Hill and a regular beating of the bounds of Roxey's tithed hayfields began. When the great tithes were not paid in 1786 the old church nearly fell to pieces. Every window was broken. Today as I wait on South Harrow Tube Station watching the swifts circle round the gasometer I sometimes look at the spire on the hilltop and before I am whisked away by electricity into darkness I sing to myself

" Hay from Roxey's spreading meadows
helped to build proud Herga's spire."

It was warm work cutting the hays and building the steeple, but it was a worth while job. Where there is no vision the levelling bulldozers triumph. The parish and the people perish, but truth cannot die. The steeple remains and Roxey—good old Roxey! is coming back.

KING STEPHEN'S MOAT AT ROXETH GRANGE

The following extracts from the Victoria County History of Middlesex—Page 4 and from the Royal Commission on Historical Monuments in England—Middlesex volume, Page 67 illustrate how miserably Harrow has failed to safeguard one of its four scheduled ancient monuments.

Victoria History (1911)

(1) " On the west side of the hill on the lower ground of the slope and west of the Northolt Road a small moat remains *in perfect state* in the grounds of The Grange. It is square with slightly rounded angles twenty feet wide between the sloping banks which gently rise to four feet six inches above the water."

Inventory of Historical Monuments in Middlesex (1937)

(2) " Homestead Moat N.W of Northolt Road and 1150 yards S.W of the church was formerly rectangular but *has been filled in* except for a small part of the S.E. arm which now forms a pond."

Middlesex—The Jubilee booklet of the County Council 1889—1939 p. 72 also makes mention of this moat and the 1897 Ordinance Map shows the size, shape and position of this moat.

PROGRESS

In his introduction to " At the Turn of the Tide " Richard Perry writes " No longer does a man plant a wood and watch with pride from year to year how it grows fine for his sons and grandsons ; instead he hacks it down and builds a row of villas in three months which is a slum in a generation. The curses of future generations despoiled of their inheritance will lie heavy on those who are destroying not only the beauty but the economic soundness of the English country by their insensate greed for money".

The following extracts from Norden, Lysons, Walford and Firth show how the passage of three centuries was powerless to rob Roxeth of its natural beauty and how swift and complete has been its desecration during the present century.

Norden (1592)

" In parts of the country about Harrow the soil is excellent fat and fertile. There is a vayne of some of the best wheatland in England. Towards the time of harvest a man may behold the fields roundabout so sweetly to address themselves to the sickle and sithe with such comfortable abundance of all kinds of graine that the husbandman which watch the fruits of his labours cannot but clap his hands for joy."

Lysons (1795)

" The view towards the west and south-west which is very extensive and beautiful may be seen to greatest advantage from the churchyard where the ground declines precipitately to Roxeth Common where the scenery is very pleasing."

Walford (1896)

" Here in the neighbourhood of Harrow the fields are still green, the hedgerows fresh and the forest trees put on their summer garb as of yore and even the smaller streams which here and there expand into broad lakes and ponds are not yet forced to burrow underground. With the exception perhaps of Vienna there is no capital in Europe with scenery so beautiful and so easily accessible."

Firth (1906)

" South Harrow can only be described as a poor suburb."

Burrows (1947) Guide

" Roxeth . . . the Cinderella of Harrow . . . has been beautifully laid out."

THE HEART OF ROXETH

(Now called West Harrow Ward)

Four roads equipped with two hostellries and flanked by two more within easy walking distance meet at Roxeth Corner. On all the old deeds and maps this spot is marked as Mount Pleasant and a pleasant place it must have been for the old folk to sit at sundown and watch the children on the common as the haywains and loaded timber trucks returned from the fields and the woods to the Manor.

After the passage of home-going rooks to their mighty ancestral Roxeth rookeries, the evening chorus of blackbirds and thrushes would gradually die down ; and after several attempts to light his clay from his flint Gilbert would lay it aside and sit back to listen to the Roxeth nightingales.

" They be singing mighty foine tonight, baint they? "

" I can't say that I takes much notice of them myself but my old missus likes en. I see the swifts be still circling round the barn."

" Yes and they will be circling round these parts long after you and I are gone. God buries his workmen but He carries on his handiwork. You are a craftsman, Jock. Did you ever look at a swift's wing?"

" No, I can't say that I have, but I once picked up a little bat that had somehow got his leathern wings scorched in my forge."

The bats and swifts career round Mount Pleasant, Gilbert and Jock retire to their cottages ; and for the next two hours the owls at the Manor tour the corn ricks and busy themselves carrying mice to their owlets high up in the old Barn. Then away in the darkness and in the distance the rumbling and creaking of a belated " TIMBER CARRIAGE " is heard. It stops for a while at the horsepond on the unfenced common and then by the light of the HALF MOON the driver discovers that his leading WHITE HORSE is going lame. It has only THREE HORSE SHOES. Only the nightingales and one kindly eavesdropper know what Ambrose the driver said that night when he failed to wake Jock Nobes the Farrier. Ambrose and Jock and Gilbert have now been resting for over two centuries in the churchyard. Jock was always a heavy sleeper and while he sleeps the tireless swifts circle round that modern utilitarian monstrosity—the Roxeth Gasometer.

What happened that night at the Manor and on each of the other nights since Thane Werenberht exchanged " his land with fields, woods and meadows at a place men call Hroces-Seath " Friends of Roxeth " are slowly finding out.

" FRIENDS OF ROXETH "

are pledged to uphold the good name of Roxeth by studying its history and boundaries and by working to maintain open spaces, good fellowship, beauty and happy children within its borders. The Registrar Treasurer is Mrs. Sherwood, " The Highlands," London Road, Harrow-on-the-Hill.

You can Help them

" *He does not die that can bequeath*
Some influence to the land he knows
Or dares, persistent, interweath
Love permanent with the wild hedgerows."

CHAPTER THIRTEEN

ROXETH'S CENTENARY

THE Eleventh Centenary of the emergence of Roxeth into history was made the occasion of local celebrations on the 8th, 9th, 10th and 11th of November, 1945. The four day programme included morning and afternoon lectures in schools on "Roxeth down the Ages" and evening lectures by P. Davenport, T. L. Bartlett and F. Hall on "The Manor Rolls," "The Story of Roxeth" and "The Planning of Roxeth" at St. Paul's Hall, Corbins Lane. Three performances of "The Thane of Roxey" were given and two thousand Centenary Leaflets were distributed. The Harrow Urban District Council marked the occasion by reinstating two of Roxeth's ancient boundary stones. They are inscribed "Roxeth 845 A.D." On Sunday, 11th November, special services were held in seven Roxeth churches and after the bounds of the parish had been beaten by Roxeth Rovers, a Community Gathering presided over by the Chairman of the Harrow Urban District Council was held round the new boundary stone at the bottom of the Long Mile. At 9 a.m. on Sunday, 11th November, 1945 a company of Roxeth Rovers assembled at the bottom of the Long Mile and noted with satisfaction that the Harrow Urban District Council had placed a new boundary stone on the old site. This new stone was well beaten :

"Oh yes! Oh yes! Oh yes! HROCES-SEATH, Roxey, Roxeth. R O X E Y. Roxeth!!"

The ancient stream which once marked the boundary, gurgled its approval from deep underground. Not far from this meeting point of Roxeth, Eastcote and Northolt, grew the ancient Ascot Bushe or Holy Thorn from which the Hundred of Elthorne (Hele Thorn) took its name.

From Ascot Bushe to Heggestone the bounds of Roxey run. These bounds were laid down by the Romans possibly during the procuratorship of Frontinus and they bear the imprint of Roman straightness. The Long or Straight Mile ran across the Roxeth marshes and through Roxeth Grange towards the Hearge or shrine on the Hill-top and it served as verge or boundary between the tythings of Newton and Dobbs. Looking up the Long Mile I like to forget the houses and picture Newton and Dobbs as two great unhedged fields, full of folk from whom the hay-wains of Hamo and

Hugh of Roxesie are collecting produce to take to the Tythe Barn, to pay for a new steeple for Harrow Church.

Leaving the old site and the new stone the beaters proceeded eastward past the field in which Wilbur Wright crashed and the crab apple tree in which a great grey shrike used to perch. Passing under the bridge and up the hill we came to the line of the boundary elms which run northwards across Northolt Park. It was interesting to note that an oak, now about fifty years old had been planted (probably by Northolt beaters) on their side of the road in continuation of the long straight line of elms. This is fortunate as only odd pieces of the granite stone near the corner pond now remain.

With permission from the Army Authorities we made our difficult way over guns and massed army equipment beating the boundary elms as we went. At the point where Dobbs Mill Lane terminated in a gate, a sunken trackway used to run eastward and then south–ward through blackberry bushes and fields, to join up with Chavel Lane, the old route to Uxbridge.

At the foot of Petts Hill, near the entrance gates to Northolt Park, we found the second of the Roxeth centenary stones set up by the Harrow Urban District Council. It was smaller than the ancient granite block which used to stand so picturesquely on the corner of the lane near Stroud Gate.

> "The boundaries of Roxeth are long and known and straight.
> They run by elm and oak and brook from Stroud to Roxboro Gate."

The road from Stroud Gate ran first through Roxeth Green which ended near Mount Pleasant (now called Roxeth Corner) then across Roxeth Common (now called Harrow School Cricket Ground) and past the Horsepond between Roxeth Farm (remaining) and Roxeth House (demolished), to Roxey Boro' Gate. As this road was the main artery, not the boundary of Roxeth, we crossed it after we had given the new stone a sound beating. Passing along the crest of the 200 contour between Stroud Gate and Woodend we crossed the L.N.E.R. near the site of Dobbs Mill, in which it is said Roxeth corn was ground for use by Tudor royalty. As we went we talked about Geoffrey de Mandeville and his holdings and poachings in Roxeth; and being joined by the Saxon children, Benedictine monks, and other relics of bygone days, we came by an ancient path to a closed up hedge. Here our passage was challenged by Keeper Feasey, but as he had himself in the days of his youth beaten the bounds of Northolt from the White Hart to Broomhill, he made a gap in the hedge of the Recreation Ground for us and the beating of the boundary oaks began:

"Oh yes! Oh yes! but who are these gathering round the ancient oak which separates the manors of Roxeth and Northolt and the hundreds of Elthorne and Gore? Oh yes! Oh yes! Oh yes! It is Sir Nicholas, Lord of the Manors of Roxeth and Northolt.

He has picked up his head at Tyburn and ridden back down the centuries to be present at our ceremony. Three cheers for Sir Nicholas! Lord of the Manor of Roxeth and four times Lord Mayor of London! "

Behind him rides one more ancient. It is Weremberht of Roxeth the King's Thane. To greet him appear a company of Benedictine monks and children led by Abbot Werhard, prepotens in Anglia. He is carrying a parchment sealed by Archbishop Ceolnoth and dated 8th November, 845. This is read by the Thane and then ceremoniously nailed to the memorial oak—" This is a day, Thane Weremberht, which in your house and in Roxeth must be long remembered " : and all the assembled friends of Roxeth said " Amen".

Then while some beaters continued their beating and the curtain dipped on eleven centuries of history, others dispersed to the seven churches which be in Roxeth : Christ Church, Salvation Army, Baptist, St. Pauls, St. Gabriels, Methodist and St. Andrews. In each of these the Elder Brethren and the XIth Centenary of Roxeth were being remembered. A diminished company of beaters proceeded almost unnoticed, from oak to oak up to Broom hill, where Mr. J. N. Stuart, the people's warden, received beaters in the days not long gone by. Then on and on, following the oaks through private fields and gardens till they came again to Mount Park Road opposite " The Oaks". There is a boundary stone marked H.P. 1847, on the lawn of Oakhurst the home of The Gardners and someday a stone or plaque should be set up near The Oaks to mark the deepest penetration of the Hundred of the Holy Thorn into the Hundred of Spears (Helethorne into Gara). Nearby is the Round Tower which has been wrongly and indifferently called " Prior Bolton Ark " and " The Duke of Wellington's Look-out". Camden 1695 writes :—" Harrow-on-the-Hill being the highest ground in the whole county was therefore made choice of by William Bolton the last prior of St. Bartholomew's in Smithfield to build him a house on, to preserve him from a Deluge which was prognosticated from certain eclipses in watery signs and was to happen in the year 1524."

By agreement with the Incumbent of Roxeth Church the old closed footpath leading downhill to Roxeth Church was open. So passing south of Les Buttez in Roxeth, Le Ermitage and the site of Betsy Wootton's less ancient Turnpike and Horse Pound we arrived at Roxeth Church just in time for the Eleven o'clock Silence, and participated in the XIth Centenary Service in this beautiful little church. " Let us now remember famous men and our fathers that begat us." The preacher was the Headmaster of Harrow.

After divine service the beaters proceeded round Roxeth Hill playground, over the fence, into an orchard and so out to the 5th Boundary stone opposite John Lyon School, midway between houses where Kingsley lived in Roxeth and Matthew Arnold in

(*Photo by* Ken Piper)

Concluding Ceremony of Roxeth's XI Centenary

(*Photo by* Ken Piper)

Weremberht and Brembre at the Centenary Pageant

(*Photo by* F. White)

Roxeth Farm (Woodbridges)

(*Photo by* F. White).

No. 5 Boundary Stone at Roxeth Mead, Middle Road

Harrow. This stone, at which Roxeth and Harrow meet was given a token beating at 12.45 p.m. and a rousing one at 1.45 p.m. when the beaters had reassembled.

So as to reach the Long Mile (Ascot Bush) No. 1 Stone by 3 o-clock the beating of Roxborough or Heath tything was abandoned and the parish, instead of the hamlet, boundaries were followed to the 8th (Pinner) Stone at the " Bridge in the Fields". Up to 1850 Mr. Joseph Greenhill and Mr. John Hodson, the farmers of Honeybun and Roxborough were listed in the Roxeth directory.

On the Harrow district enclosure map the steep path at the side of John Lyon School, and its continuation " Jolly's Alley", are marked " Footway." Using this old footway, and passing the built up site of Dudley Lodge with its happy memories of dancing on the lawn and flower shows we searched in vain for " The Spring in the Fields." This source of the Roxbourne was possibly the " Seath " which gives us the second syllable of HROCES-SEATH (Roxeth), and here, according to whichever derivation of the name is accepted, the Rooks drank or the mythological HROC lived. Like the Common Pond, St. Edmunds Pond and the pump at the top of West Street, " The Spring " had disappeared.

This spring of good drinking water used to mark the beginning of the " Mediæval Hedge," which hindered geese, swine or mangy horses wandering from Roxeth Common into Roxeth's cultivated long strip Common Fields. It also served as a boundary between Newton and Heath tything. It was not easy to trace the line of the Mediæval Hedge through modern suburbia. This line is clearly marked on Hugh Brauns map of Mediæval Harrow, and it is also shewn as the northern boundary of the ecclesiastical parish of Roxeth.

At different times Roxeth has been three possedas in a Roman pagus, a vil, a manor, three tythings, a hamlet and an ecclesiastical parish. At a division of the H.U.D.C. area into wards the name Roxeth was given to the Dobbs Field Area and the heart and core of Roxeth was given the modern railway station naming West Harrow. Fortunately the old name survives at Roxeth Corner ; and as some of the Roxeth boundaries follow geometric lines laid down by Roman surveyors, they cannot be lost when boundary stones disappear, or when boundary trees are cut down to make room for Prison Camps or much needed houses.

When the beaters arrived at the Footpath Bridge over the tube railway they noted with regret that the white wooden triangular post which used to mark the bounds of Roxeth and Pinner had disappeared. From this point the land slopes away in all directions, and as a line from the Long Mile Boundary Stone through this spot points straight to a Roman measuring or Hedding stone at Headstone, this would have been a very suitable place for the Roman surveyor to set up his instruments and note the lay of the land.

At this point the Mediæval Hedge ended, and here the Roxeth parish boundary line turns sharply southward. Fortunately a few ancient elms have survived to line out Roxeth's western boundary. In 1945 this line ran across allotments; in 1948 it runs across the roofs of a modern prefab settlement. According to Montagu Sharpe's illustration, the Roxeth boundary line runs along a very ancient survey line. These boundary elms have also long been known to bird watchers as the nesting quarters of Roxeth's largest colony of tree sparrows (Passus m. montanus).

After beating the bounds on the Bridge, twelve Roxeth Rovers (two of them just returned from the wars) gave the boundary elm opposite the Italians' Orderly Room a proper bastinado :—" Oh yes! Oh yes! Oh yes! Sesta Feneesh! Hroces-Seath! Roxey! Roxeth!" Then we climbed a fence and went singing along the western side of the Roxbourne, passing near the site of the Victorian Shooting Butts and the still more ancient site of the Battle of the Bonefield.

For years these fields (and the Priors Fields half-way to Hayes) sheltered hundreds of snipe and corncrakes and here in the fall thousands of lapwings and scores of golden plover assembled. After passing through a square mile of solid surburbia we were glad to emerge into Field End Lane (formerly Bourne Lane), near the old Bourne Farm Cottages.

Then with a last beating of Bench Mark 120 loud enough to awaken the crowd which has assembled on the Long Mile Roundabout, the Roxey boys arrived singing at the New Boundary Stone. For the second time that day they gave it a sound beating : " Oh yes! Oh yes! Oh yes! proclaimed Beadle Sampson and with a ringing of the bell and a beating of withies the beaters replied, " Hroces-Seath, Roxey. Roxeth, R O X E Y, Roxeth!"

Then at 3.30 p.m. when the choirs of churches and representation of Roxeth Societies and associations had assembled on the greensward, Mr. F. A. Coles, Chairman of the Harrow Urban District Council, called on all present to remember Weremberht and Werhard, Lanfranc and Anselm, Hugh and Hamo, Nicholas Brembre and all those humble folk who right down the ages had upheld the good name of Roxeth.

The Toc H Lamp was lit. The Legion wreath of poppies pressed on to the New Boundary Stone and with the response " We will remember them," the Hroces-Seath Centenary Celebrations concluded.

CHAPTER FOURTEEN

A ROXETH CHRONOLOGY

"Full fathom five thy father lies, of his bones are coral made."

A deposit of London clay as deep as the Roxeth gasometer is high (245 feet) covers Roxeth. Beneath this a strata of chalk 200 feet thick goes down to meet the impervious layer of gault which covers our primary rock foundations. The arrangement of these stratas shews that although Roxeth has been submerged several times by the ocean it has always risen again.

B.C.

100 The Catevellauni, a powerful tribe from Chalons, settled in the district and established their Wilde Beaste Park at Ruislip and their strongholds at St. Albans and Brockley Hill.

55 Julius Ceasar passed this way.

A.D.

74–78 Julius Frontinus Procurator. Boundaries for Middlesex and Roxeth planned.

407 Romans leave Britain.

597 Augustine arrives.

604 Mellitus the local bishop christianised local heathen shrines like Ascot Bush.

704 First mention of Middlesex.

767 Offas grant of land and a house.

825 Archbishop Wulfred acquired Harrow from the Lady Cwoenthwyth.

830 Werhard—prepotens in Anglia reinstated monks in domain of which they had been deprived.

832 Werhard's Will.

845 The HROCES-SEATH parchment signed by an Archbishop, eight Bishops, a Thane (Weremberht) and an Abbot (Werhard).

840–850 Middlesex disturbed by Danes. Battles may have been fought at Haest Hill and Bonefield. Rox-Borough may be a Danish name.

878 Watling Street boundary agreed by Alfred and Guthrum.

946 First record of Preston.

1016 King Canute and Edmund Ironside pass this way. "There cannot be two Kings of Brentford."

1066 Earl Leofwine the local landlord dies at the Battle of Hastings.
William I passes this way. A column of his forces moves up from Battersea through Hayes and Roxeth to Harrow.

1070.c. Geoffrey de Mandeville goes poaching.

1086 Detailed account of the district in the Doomsday record.

1094 Harrow Church consecrated by Anselm.

1145.c. King Stephen at Roxeth.

1170 Becket's third and last visit to his Manor House, 12th to 17th December.

1205 Lands of Ralph de Rokesheye (Roxeth) conveyed to Roger de la Dune, Constable of the Tower of London.

1206 King John takes Harrow from Stephen Langton and keeps his greyhounds there.

1237.c Roxeth hay included in endowment of Harrow Vicarage. Hamo de Rokesheye one of the signatories.

1246 Elevation of relics of St. Edmund at Pontigny.

1290–1306 Edward I passes this way (six times).

1302 Archbishop Winchelsea holds ordination in his chapel at Harrow.

1324 John de Roxe, a juror at Endowment enquiry.

1344 Acquisition of Headstone Manor by the Archbishops.

1349 (November). Oldest surviving record of Court of Rectory Manor.

1384 John Intowne's son educated against the will of his Lord.

1371–1389 Sir Nicholas Brembre, Lord of the Manor of Roxeth in succession to William the Outlaw.

1392 'Les Buttez' in Roxeth mentioned.

1400 Inventory of Archbishop Arundel's property including 'The Grange,'

1424 Roxeth has three Tything men.

1425 John Roxeth caught eavesdropping.

1456 John Lyon admitted to John Greenhill's lands at Roxeth.

1462 Joan Sextane of 'Le Alehoope', Roxeye, fined 2d.

1475 Five sellions of land in Pynner and Roxeth transferred.

1503 Fishing in Roxeth Common Pond forbidden.

1521 William Cox's mangey horse on Roxey Common.

1535 Henry VIII goes hunting and meets Wolsey at Harrow.

1545 Cranmer surrenders the Manors of Harrow to Henry VIII.

1547 Henry VIII grants them to Sir Edward North.

1550 Henri Bette of Le Ermitage presented for overflowing of St. Edmund's Pond.

Roxeth Corner, 1909

Northolt Road, 1912

21st Reunion of 12th Harrow Scouts, 27.5.45

(*Photo by* W. Barns, Peterboro Road)

Roxborough Farm on Site Opposite Butler Avenue

1565	Edmund Robertes sells farm in Roxsey.
	Thomas Blunt baptised.
1572	John Lyon obtains his charter.
1586	William Greenhill of Roxey a Governor of Harrow School.
1603	Queen Elizabeth dies.
1613	Death of Katherine Clerk.
1615	Thomas Page of Roxey builds Harrow School.
1627	George Ashwell of Roxey published his Theological Books.
1629	Court Roll order to pull down erections on the Lord's waste at Roxeth.
1630	Sale of Roxeth Manor to Thomas Hutchinson (7th and 8th January).
1637	Local Ship Money prosecutions.
1646	Charles I passes this way (27th April).
1660	Payments to six good wives for teaching poor of Roxeth, Wembley, Sudbury and Harrow.
1681	Survey of waste lands at Roxeth.
1706	Thomas Brian of Roxey Manor prentices John Wilde.
1714	Queen Anne dies.
1745	Rocque's Map of Middlesex.
1764	Perceval Hart takes over Roxeth Grange Manor from Brian Taylor.
1771	Governor's coach wrecked on Roxeth Common.
1703–1791	The Century of Wesley.
1786	Not a pane of glass left in Harrow Church.
1800	George III passes this way.
1801	Turnpike Road to London opened.
1803	Roxeth Common enclosed.
1811	Canal Boat Passenger services Greenford Road to Paddington.
1831	Census of the hamlets of Roxeth and Harrow.
1837	First train service London to Weald (..Wealdstone).
1848	Queen Victoria at the Peachey Stone.
1849	Enquiry into sanitation of the hamlets of Roxeth and Harrow.
1850	Harrow on the Hill Local Board of Health area incorporates Roxeth.
1860	Roxeth's Great Barn used as a theatre.
1863	Roxeth becomes an ecclesiastical parish.
1880	Metropolitan Railway runs to Harrow.
1894	H.U.D.C. formed.
1901	Queen Victoria dies.
1903	23rd June, Electric trains run to a station called South Harrow.
1934	Greater Harrow administrative area formed.
1945	Roxeth celebrates its XIth Centenary.

CHAPTER FIFTEEN

GUIDE AND DIRECTORY TO PAST AND PRESENT ROXETH

ROXETH COMMUNITIES. The first Roxeth community may have grown up round the fresh water source of the ROXBOURNE and the fertile ground between the wooded hilltop and the Roxeye marshes was probably the first area to be cultivated. Under changing clerical and lay landlords the area near ROXETH CORNER remained the centre of the Roxeth community.

Roxeth may have owed the draining of its marshes and the sensible three fold division of its lands to a Saxon community of CHRIST CHURCH monks. This would account for the enduring interest of the Rectors and the Christ Church trustees in NEWTON FIELD.

The lay community which worked the three tythings may have lived just south of the Brothers settlement ; as from an early date the huts of these cultivators and the marshes beyond them were known as ROXEYE.

Under the Manorial system of Government the Roxeth community was represented at the Harrow Manor Court by three tything men (NEWTON, DOBBS, and HEATH) one from each of the three great COMMON FIELD areas.

The communal development of these three Roxeth Common Field areas continued long after the break up of the Mediæval Manor System ; and even after Roxeth was stripped of its Common and its Common Fields, its identity as a HAMLET with a strong community spirit (good old Roxey) persisted.

In 1863 Roxeth became an ecclesiastical PARISH with bounds almost as extensive, but different from, those of the old hamlet. In place of Roxeth Common and Roxborough, a large area round Greenford Road was incorporated in the Roxeth parish. This area has since been restored to St. Andrews, Sudbury.

In this present century a rapid development of the entire Roxeth area, combined with a use of railway station namings for nebulous areas seemed for a while to dilute the community spirit and to shatter the ancient three ward unity of the old Hamlet ; but the success of the Eleventh Centenary Celebrations proved that this was not the case, and FRIENDS of ROXETH have now pledged themselves " to uphold the good name of ROXETH by studying its boundaries and history and by working to preserve open spaces, good fellowship, beauty and happy children within its borders."

BOUNDARIES. The boundaries of the old hamlet, the location of the old Manor Site, the old village, the three tything areas—Newton, Dobbs and Heath, and the position of eight of the old boundary marks (1) Ascot Bushe (2) Northolt Stone (3) Stroud Gate (4) Les Buttez (5) Harrow Stone (6) Roxboro' Gate (7) Heggestone (8) Pinnerstone are shewn on the map "Roxeth before The Railways." (See front end papers.)

OLD ROADS and LANES. (1) Roxeth Road or Lower Roxeth Road ran from Roxeth Corner to Roxborough Gate. It is now called Lower Road as far as the Horse trough ; and thence to Roxborough Bridge, Bessborough Road, after F. Ponsonby, the Harrovian Cricketer who became Earl of Bessborough, (2) Middle Roxeth Road (now Middle Road) ran up from Roxeth Corner and forked into Hog or Hogarth Lane (now Crown Street) and Byron Hill, (3) London Hill (now Roxeth Hill) also ran up from Roxeth Corner towards the old Butts, the Toll Gate, and the Horse Pound. (4) Mount Park and South Hill Avenue were often called the Toll Gate Roads, (5) Roxeth Green (now Northolt Road) extended from Roxeth Corner to Stroud Gate, (6) Dobbs Mill Lane (now serves as the main approach to Northolt Park Race course), (7) The Long Mile (now Eastcote Lane) began at The Postes (now Woolworths) and ended at, (8) Bourne Lane (now Field End Road) (9) Pinner Lane (now Rayners) was a saxon trackway, linking the ancient settlements of Roxeth and Pinner.

Coming from Roxeth Corner on the west side of Northolt Road were (10) Mount Pleasant Lane (11) The Grange Drive (12) East croft Lane (now absorbed in The Gas Works) (13) and (14) Stanley and Sherwood—the new roads—then came the Long Mile (15) St. Hildas Drive (16) Valentine Road (17) Barnetts (now Corbins Lane) (18) Grove or Grove Farm Lane (now Park Lane).

From Roxeth Corner on the East of Northolt Road were, (19) Waldron Yard, (20) Grange Road, (21) Alma Road, (22) Toll Gate Road, (now South Hill Avenue).

HOUSES and FARMS in old Roxeth (A) Between Roxboro Gate and Stroud Gate. (1) Roxborough Farm, (2) Honeybun Farm, (3) (N) Roxeth Farm or Woodbridges, (4) Roxeth House or High Capers at the corner of West Street, (5) Dudley Lodge, (6) The GRANGE with its scheduled Moat and Great Barn possibly the oldest continuously habited site in the greater Harrow area, (7) "The White Horse,"(8) "The Half Moon" took its name from the shape of the Pond over which, (9) Sladdens Stores (now Allens) was built, (10) The Timber Truck (or Carriage), (12) The Drill Hall house with Dunmore's Barn opposite, (13) "The Three Horses Shoes" complete with pond and railings and opposite, (14) Shearlocks, Roxeth's oldest established shop, (15) Eastcroft Farm up Eastcroft lane has been submerged by the Gas Work,

(16) Dodds (now "Deep Seas") was a fish and fruit, and coal shop with a Bus service, (17) James Atkins Builders Yard adjoined the Circus Field opposite the Toll Gate (now South Harrow Railway Station), (18) St. Hilda's Nursery stretched from The Postes (now Woolworths) to, (19) The Cottages, which were flanked by Parks Aviary complete with Christmas Tree (now J. Massey and Sons) and Mrs. Underwood's shop (now the Roxeth Civic Restaurant), (20) Barnett's or Roxeth Farm remains. It looked out between its great Lombardy poplars not on "The Odeon" but on one great field, "The Park," which stretched from The Toll Gate road to Jim Atkin's field (*i.e.* from the District Railway to the hedge at the rear of Welldon Park School). In this Park the Drag Hunts and Jubilee Procession assembled, and from it Charles Fleet made Balloon ascents), (21) Grove Farm Dairy (now The Paddocks) (22) A picture book Cottage complete with duck pond and pear tree in the centre of a field (now half up Woodend Avenue), (23) Parkers Farm (wrongly called Parkhurst Farm by those who developed, the site now quite appropriately named Stroud Gate). This was the last house in Roxeth before the boundary stone was reached at the foot of Petts Hill.

(B) Interesting buildings up Roxeth Hill were, (24) The Wooden Salvation Army Barracks, (25) Roxeth Vicarage and Church, (26) The Butts, adjoining Betsy Wootens Cottage and the Horse Pound. (C) Down the Long Mile (now Eastcote Lane) were, (27) Temples Orchard Farm (now Beechwood Avenue), (28) Tythe Barn and Farm, (29) Dabbs Hill (formerly Dobbs Mill) Lodge the home of the Greatorex children who planted interesting trees in the middle of their fields. (now the Bus Stop at the junction of Walton Avenue and Eastcote Lane).

OLD ROXETH NAMES. (1) ROXBOROUGH may imply a Danish settlement or the burial place of HROC. (2) ROXETH the rooks drinking place or the abode of HROC. (3) ROXBOURNE, the rooks (or HROCS) stream. (4) ROXEY (e) . . the high ground or spot above the marshes, perhaps the early embanked stockaded village. (5) NEWTON an exceptionally large Common Field area or tything along the Roxbourne between the Bonefield and the Long Mile. (6) DOBBS, (later Dabbs) another great Common Field area east of the Long Mile, gave its name to Dabbs Mill (near Northolt Park Station), Dobbs Mill Lane and Dobbs Hill Lodge. (7) HEATH field or Hill field, the nearest tything to the Manor Site, a name also used for the area beyond the Common as far as Roxborough Gate. (8) BONEFIELD—on the far side of the Roxbourne—is the site of a forgotten battle. (9) ROXETH GROVE—a wood and a mansion are shewn in old maps on the present Alexandra Park area. (10) Roxeth Green stretched from (11) Stroud Gate to (12) Roxeth Common. (13) Mount Park. Did London's ancient hunting rights penetrate to this hawking Mount and hunting Parc.

Harrow, Pinner, Roxeth, Weald, and Stanmore each have their

treasured place names and traditions ; but the too easy acceptance of railway and meaningless names is depriving new residents of an interest and pride in their home districts. The Harrow Urban District Council has to cover a very big field but before providing fifteen brand new Community Centres it might be well advised to consider what could be achieved by (1) A Greater Harrow Pageant. (2) the teaching of local history in schools, (3) the appointment of an advisory Place and Street naming committee.

THE HARROW URBAN DISTRICT was formed on 4th January, 1934 by the amalgamation of Harrow on the Hill U.D., Wealdstone U.D. and Hendon R.D. Its area is 12,558 acres. Its population in 1947 was estimated at 217,810, and its rateable value on 1st January, 1948 at £2,171,656.

The old geographical and communal five fingered unity of Greater Harrow has been partly concealed by a modern utility glove overmarked with railway lines and railway names.

The five major divisions of greater Harrow are (1) The Hill with Greenhill and Kenton making the palm and thumb and (2) Roxeth, (3) Pinner, (4) Weald, (5) Stanmore making up the projecting fingers.

The three ancient Roxeth tythings or common field divisions, Newton, Dobbs and Heath, survive under the ward names Roxbourne, Roxeth and West Harrow.

ROXBOURNE Ward (Newton Field Area) is enclosed by the Picadilly Railway, the Eastcote boundary line and Eastcote Lane. It has an AREA of 475 acres, an ELECTORATE of 10,088 in 1948, and a RATEABLE VALUE of £104,629.

ROXETH Ward (Dobbs Field Area) is enclosed by the Picadilly line, the Northolt Boundary and Eastcote Lane. It has an AREA of 559 acres, an ELECTORATE of 11,715, and a RATEABLE VALUE of £164,647.

WEST Harrow Ward (old Roxeth area minus its Parish Church) is enclosed by the main Roxeth road, (now called Northolt Road—Lower Road—Roxborough Road), and the converging Metropolitan and Picadilly lines going towards Uxbridge. It has an AREA of 555 acres, an ELECTORATE of 11,329, and a RATEABLE VALUE of £124,828.

When the Harrow Urban District Council is redivided into three Divisions, the present Roxeth and Roxbourne wards will be included in The West Harrow Division and the present West Harrow (..old Roxeth) ward will be in the Central Harrow Division.

PUBLIC SERVICES

Harrow Urban District Council.

Chairman 1947—1948, L. Cridford, J.P.

Clerk of the Council (H. Wells), Harrow Weald Lodge, Harrow.

Engineer and Surveyor (H. W. Rackham). Public Health (E. W. Caryl Thomas), Council Offices, Stanmore.

District Education Officer (A. G. Field), and Youth Officer (Miss R. Anderson), High Street, Harrow.

Middlesex County Council, Guildhall, Westminster S.W.1, is now The Education, the Public Assistance and the Sanitation authority for the district.

Food Office, 380 Northolt Road (Byron 4620).

National Registration Office, Dominion Cinema (Harrow 3217).

Police, X Division, 76 West Streets Harrow (Byron 1113).

Harrow Hospital, Roxeth Hill (Byron 2232).

Citizens Advice Bureau, St. Hildas Hall, Northolt Road and S.S.A.F.A. (Tuesday and Thursday mornings).

Roxeth Civic Restaurant, Northolt Road.

Schools. The Council Schools are situated at Roxeth Hill, Eastcote Lane, Wynenhoe Road (Welldon Park), Torbay Road (Roxbourne), and Vaughan Road.

Stations on L.N.E.R. named Sudbury Hill, and Northolt Park. On Metropolitan named West Harrow and Rayners Lane. On Piccadilly Tube named Sudbury Hill, South Harrow, Rayners Lane.

Buses along the Northolt Road, 114, Edgware to Rayners Lane, 140, Hayes or Northolt to Mill Hill, 158, Watford or Harrow Weald to Ruislip, 187, Hampstead to South Harrow.

Post Offices: 1. Roxeth, Roxeth Corner. 2. South Harrow, Northolt Road. 3. Alexandra Avenue.

CINEMAS. Odeon, (Roxeth Ward) 337 Northolt Road. Odeon (Roxbourne Ward) near Rayners Lane Station.

BANKS. Barclays, 192 Northolt Road. Lloyds, 254 Northolt Road. Midland, 235 Northolt Road.

NEWSPAPERS. Harrow Observer and Gazette, 323 Station Road, Harrow. The Middlesex Advertiser, 69 Roxborough Road.

OPEN SPACES. Roxeth Recreation Ground, 17 acres. Alexandra Park, 21 acres. West Harrow Recreation Ground, 26 acres and ALLOTMENTS near Roxeth Recreation Ground ; Newton Farm ; and opposite Roxeth Gas Works.

PLACES OF WORSHIP.

Church of England. Christ Church, Roxeth Hill ; St. Pauls, Corbins Lane ; St. Peters, Sumner Road ; St. Andrews, Roseberry Avenue.

Baptist. St. Hildas, Northolt Road.

Methodist. Walton Avenue, Eastcote Lane.

St. Gabriels (R.C.) Northolt Road.

Salvation Army, Roxeth Hill.

CLUBS AND SOCIETIES.

Ancient order of Foresters, 81 Northolt Road.

British Legion Club, Northolt Road, Roxeth.

Chaffinch Community Centre, The Vicarage, Corbins Lane.

Eastwood Lawn Tennis Club, Eastcote Avenue.

Friends of Roxeth, 91 Woodend Avenue, Roxeth.

Roxeth Boy Scouts Local Association, 100A Roxeth Green Avenue.

Roxeth and Harrow Church Lads Brigade, Northolt Road,
Roxeth Bowls Club meet Roxeth Recreation Ground.
Roxeth Parish Hall and Sunday School, Northolt Road, Roxeth.
South Harrow and Roxeth Ratepayers' Association, 27 Sandringham Cresent.
Toc H., Harrow, meets, 6 Crown Street. Thursdays at 8 p.m.
Tythe Farm Social Club, Tythe Farm, Eastcote Lane.
Workers' Educational Association (123 Park Lane.)

SHOPS

How Roxeth's village green has changed in the past century can be guessed by comparing the Traders listed in Chapters 5 and 10 with the following list of a few of the 500 shops and establishments which now have frontages along Northolt Road.

Northolt Road—South Side (Nos.1—501).

A. G. Mendham, Off License and The Half Moon at Roxeth Corner; (1—5) Formerly Sladdens then Allens (site of the old Pond); (7) L. G. Clibbens; Wrights Slaughter House (formerly Wingroves and a century ago the cottage of William Martin, Pig Killer); (11—13) W. H. Cullen, Grocer; *Waldron Yard*; (15) The Timber Carriage; Roxeth and Harrow C.L.B.; Sub Fire Station (the old Mission Hall); (59) E. E. Guildford, Newsagent; *Grange Road*; (81) E. E. Hurford, Ancient Order of Foresters, Lodge 4238; (83) R.S.P.C.A.; *Alma Road*; (103) C. J. Shearlock, Grocer, Est. 1886; (109) C. E. Page, Corn Merchant; (179) Surgery of Dr. Giles and Dr. McArthur; *Brooke Avenue*; (201) E. F. Pratt, Watchmaker, Est. over 50 years; *South Hill Avenue*; South Harrow (i.e. Roxeth) Station; *Parkfield Road*; (235) Midland Bank; (2) Wright Cooper Ltd.; (3) Harold Payne, Opthalmic Optician; (5) Gas Light and Coke Show Rooms; (8—9) J. Sainsbury Ltd.; (10) Boots Chemist; *Eastcote Road*; (265—267) Geoff Ltd., Drapers; (277) H. G. Hodges Ltd., Stationers; (281) Hills Library, Booksellers; (285) Ansley Bros., Greengrocers; (295) George Porter and Co., House Furnishers; *Wargrave Road*; (337) Odeon Cinema (Manager A. M. Morrison); (343) E. A. Spires; "Genners," Sports Dealer and Confectioner; *Wyvenhoe Road*; (345) The Flower Basket; T. W. Holden, Butcher; *Woodend Avenue*; (409—423) *Westwood Avenue*; (424—453) *Stroud Gate*; Northolt Park Station; The Swan.

Northolt Road, North Side. (Nos. 2—504)

G. Bentley and Son, Hairdresser, Roxeth Corner, Est. 1886; (2) Mrs. A. S. Kelly; (2a) F. W. Simkins, Radio Supplies; *Shaftesbury Avenue*; Franklins Estate Agents; Grange Farm (Hall and Son, Dairy Farmer, Est. 1851); British Legion Club Ltd; Roxeth Sunday School and Parish Hall; Roxeth Men's Institute; The Drill Hall; (100) The Three Horse Shoes; *Eastcroft Lane*; Gas Light and Coke Works; *Stanley Road*; (168) E. F. Hatherley, Hairdresser; (170—172) T.C.R. Stores, Grocers; *Sherwood Road*; (182) J. A. Atkins and Sons, Builders, Est. 1884;

(190) E. J. Ross, Homestore Furniture Dealers ; (192) Barclays Bank ; (200) Geo. Simpson, Tobacconist ; Piccadilly Railway Arches and Market ; (236) Frederick Drake and Co, Hosiers ; (240) R. C. Frank, Chemist ; (246—248) Watford Co-operative Society Ltd ; *Eastcote Lane* ; (250) F. W. Woolworth and Co Ltd ; (254) Lloyds Bank Ltd ; Baptist Church ; Post Office ; (296) J. A. Massey and Sons, Est. 1879 ; (300) Roxeth Civic Restaurant ; *Valentine Road* ; Roxeth Farm (Barnetts) ; Odeon Car Park ; *Corbins Lane* ; The Belmont Fruit Stores ; (368) " Giffs," Motor Cycle Accessories ; (372) Mrs. M. B. Bell, Confectioner ; (380) Food Office ; Church of St. Gabriel, R.C.; (400) H. L. Hodges, Newsagent ; *Park Lane* ; George Champness, The Paddocks ; (504) Somervell Road ; L.N.E.R. Bridge ; Roxeth Boundary Stone, A.D. 845.

INDEX

Map made from section plan annexed to the

INCLOSURE AWARD OF HARROW

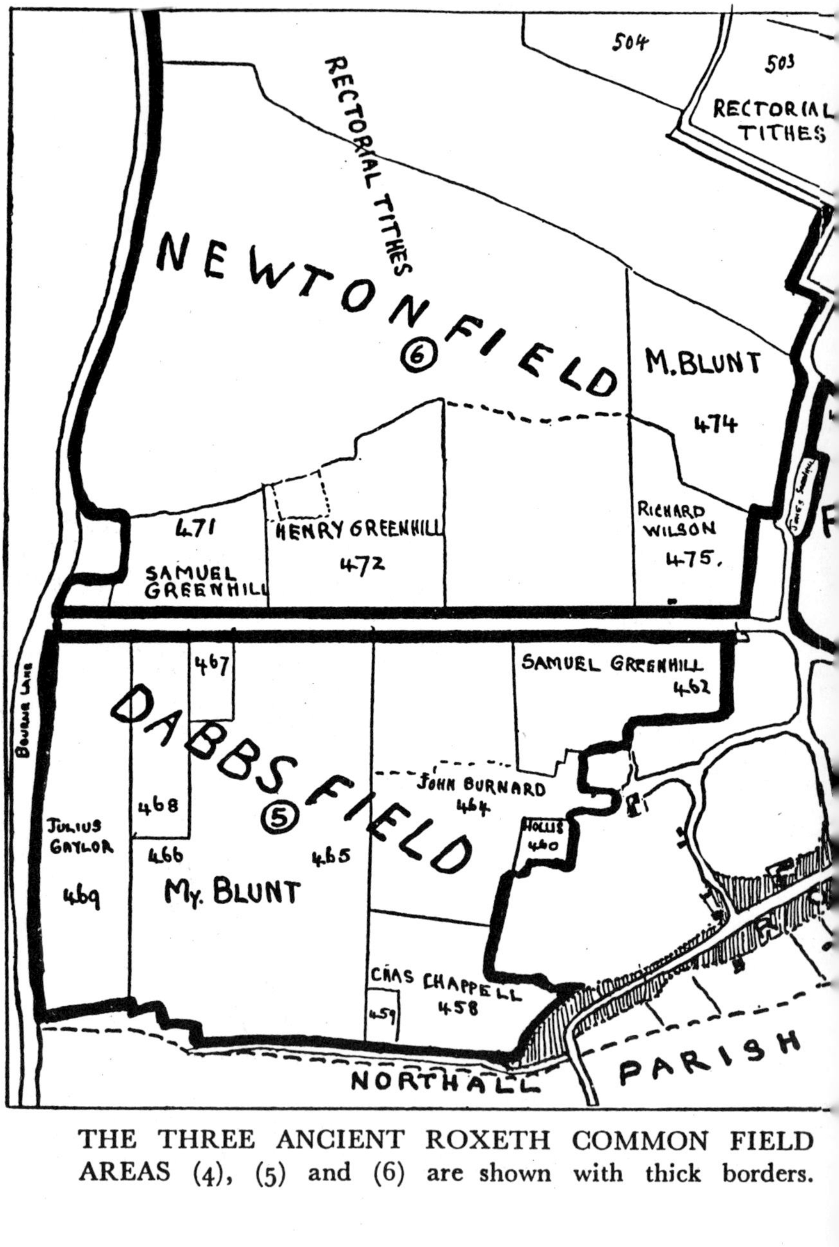

THE THREE ANCIENT ROXETH COMMON FIELD AREAS (4), (5) and (6) are shown with thick borders.

Public Records Office Reference M.R. 612.

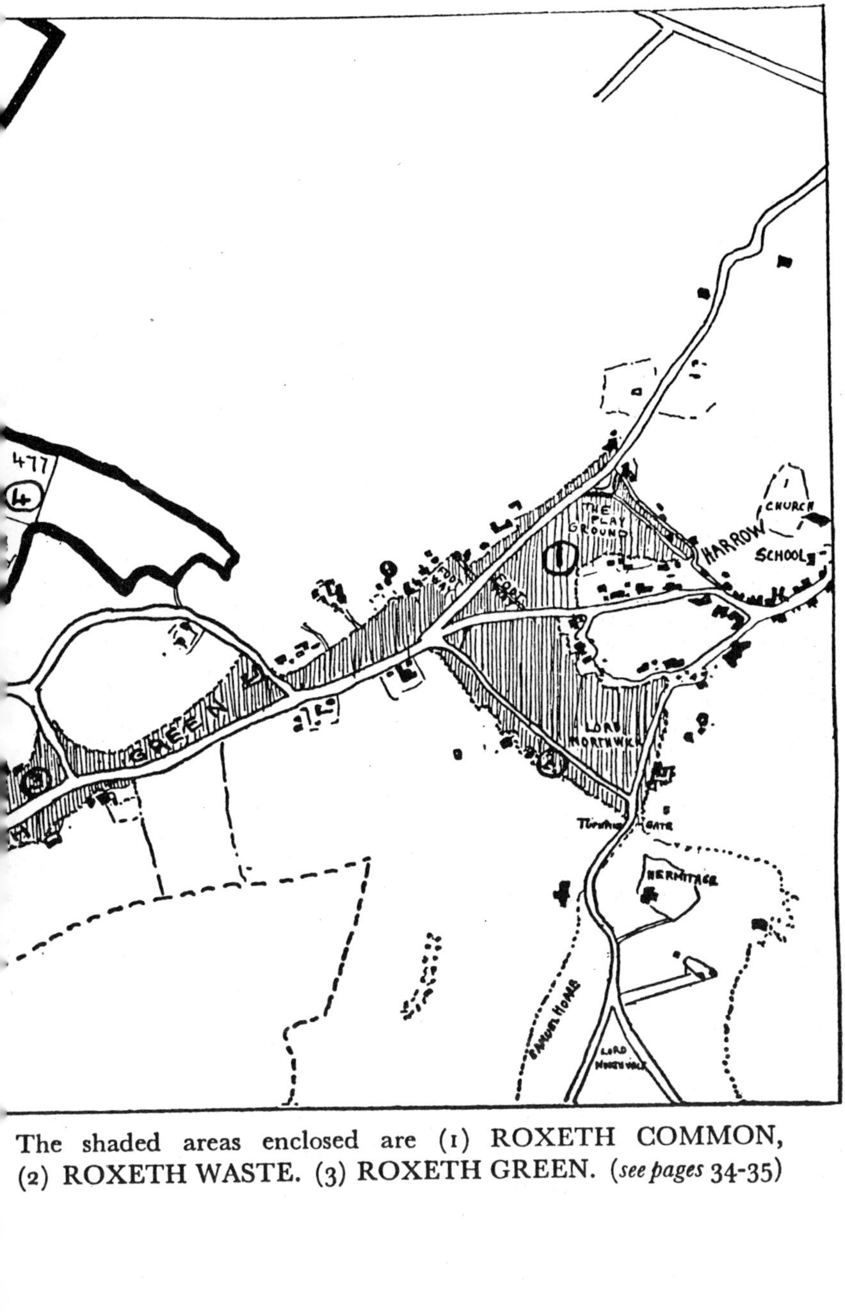

The shaded areas enclosed are (1) ROXETH COMMON, (2) ROXETH WASTE. (3) ROXETH GREEN. (*see pages* 34-35)